Acclaim for The **Wild Mushroom** Cookbook

"This delightful exploration of fungi is at once accessible and esoteric. The authors reveal forest treasures and offer them up in scrumptious dishes, from appetizers and soups to desserts. *The Wild Mushroom Cookbook* not only guides you through the preparation of mushrooms but also inspires you to get out into the wild to harvest them yourself. Keep a copy in your kitchen and buy another for your favorite mushroom lover."

— Michele Anna Jordan, Chef, author of *Vinaigrettes and Other Dressings* and *More Than Meatballs*

"If you love the thrill of the mushroom hunt and bringing back your trophies to feast on as much as I do, this is a must-have book. Chock-full of mushroom lore, serious fungi knowledge, and inspired recipes for using mushrooms in every way, Alison and Merry welcome you into their wild and adventuresome world with open arms."

— Georgeanne Brennan, author, *A Pig in Provence* and owner, La Vie Rustic

"A truly authentic West Coast gem! From soufflé to sorbet and aspics to applesauce, these amazing women bring their readers an amazing blend of fearlessly diverse culinary concepts and clear mastery of mushroom!"

— Kelly Hatcher, Chef, The Tip of the Knife

The **Wild Mushroom** Cookbook

Recipes from **Mendocino**

Alison Gardner
Merry Winslow

Alison Gardner
Merry Winslow

Illustrations by Merry Winslow

BAREFOOT
NATURALIST
PRESS

The Wild Mushroom Cookbook
Recipes from Mendocino
Copyright © 2014 by Alison Gardner and Merry Winslow

Barefoot Naturalist Press
P.O. Box 894
Mendocino, CA 95460
Cover and book design by Michael Brechner / Cypress House
Photographs and illustrations by Merry Winslow
Cover Photograph of turkey tail mushrooms by Alison Gardner

PUBLISHER'S CATALOGING-IN-PUBLICATION DATA
Gardner, Alison (Alison L.)
The wild mushroom cookbook : recipes from Mendocino / Alison Gardner and Merry Winslow. -- First edition. -- Mendocino, CA : Barefoot Naturalist Press, [2014]
    pages ; cm.
    ISBN: 978-0-9904400-0-0
    Includes index.
    Summary: The most comprehensive collection of wild mushroom recipes ever assembled in one book, from breakfast to dinner, appetizers to dessert. It also describes the best uses for different mushrooms, mentions procedures useful in their preparation, and covers the best methods of preservation for different species. Full of ideas which may also be applied to store-bought mushrooms, this book will stimulate your imagination and guide your creativity.--Publisher.
    1. Cooking (Mushrooms) 2. Cooking (Mushrooms)--California--Mendocino. 3. Edible mushrooms. 4. Edible mushrooms--California--Mendocino. 5. Cookbooks. I. Winslow, Merry. II. Title.

TX804 .G37 2014   2014948507
641.6/58--dc23   1409

Printed in the USA
2 4 6 8 9 7 5 3 1
First edition

To the memory
of Ryane Snow

Contents

Foreword

THE MENDOCINO COAST IS a magical place to see and enjoy wild mushrooms. Their abundance and variety draws visitors from all over the country. Photographers, ecologists, mycologists both professional and amateur come to this area in search of mushrooms. This book is for the "mycophagist," the person who hunts mushrooms for food and wants to find out how to prepare them.

Mushrooms play incredibly important roles in our natural ecosystems. They are food for many of our wildlife from squirrels and deer to banana slugs and insects. They are decomposers of leaf litter, manures, large woody debris and even other mushrooms. In our moist climate, they are the ultimate "recyclers". More subtle than the decomposers are the symbiotic mushrooms that contribute to forest health. These "mycorrhizal" species make up most of the large mushroom body that we see in our walks in the woods. They extend the trees' root systems to absorb more water, nutrients and they increase the trees' resistance to drought.

Please respect our natural environments and pick gently and only those specimens that you plan to eat. An entire group of mushrooms might look fine to eat but one or all may be riddled with maggots. When picking mushrooms it is best for the mushroom to be cut close to the ground so as to disturb the soil as little as possible. However, many people make sure and look for the volva of an *Amanita* first as many are toxic, and cover any mushroom remains. This is important because the fragile microscopic mycorrhizal strands grow throughout the leaf litter and are the connections to the trees that we want to protect.

Mushrooms are a delight to just look at while wandering through our majestic forests. After more than 30 years, my children still want to go mushroom hunting when they come home to visit in the fall. Finding and identifying mushrooms while walking in the forest becomes a walk of exploration full of surprises and, if you are in a permissible area, a rewarding bounty.

I would encourage all mushroom hunters to become familiar with those places one can hunt legally and safely. The largest public land open to mushroom hunters on the Mendocino Coast is the 50,000 acres of Jackson State Demonstration Forest. One can acquire maps and permits for collecting at their office on Main Street at Spruce Street in Fort Bragg. Local State Parks do not allow collecting any plant or mushrooms.

Obviously one needs to know what species to pick. Be very careful in your mushroom identification deliberations. There is not a single book published which has all of the mushroom species that you will encounter in the woods. Enjoy this lovely book full of wonderful recipes for local Mendocino Coast mushrooms!

Teresa Sholars
Professor Emeritus of Biology
College of the Redwoods
July, 2014.

The **Wild Mushroom** Cookbook

Introduction

THIS IS NOT A MUSHROOM identification book! Remember that any time you eat a wild mushroom you are staking your life on your mushroom identification skills. Make sure that you can identify the species you plan to eat with 100% certainty. As our friend Ryane Snow used to say, "There are old mushroom hunters, and bold mushroom hunters, but there are no old, bold mushroom hunters." The most poisonous mushrooms, such as some species of *Amanita*, *Galerina* and *Cortinarius*, can kill you after ingesting even a small amount. The deadly *Amanita phalloides*, the Destroying Angel, is reputed by survivors to be delicious. *Amanita* toxins will often cause stomach upset, diarrhea, and vomiting, AFTER they have moved past your stomach (when it's too late to have it pumped), followed by a cessation of these symptoms. The victim may then die week or so later of liver failure. Some toxic *Cortinarius* species do not contain gastrointestinal toxins, so you don't get sick right away, but die weeks later of kidney failure.

The majority of toxic mushroom species have just gastrointestinal toxins, which will make you throw up and/or give you diarrhea for a few hours to several days. We have heard stories of people putting misidentified mushrooms in turkey stuffing for Thanksgiving, and the guests all getting sick afterwards.

Even with a correct identification of an edible mushroom, it is still quite possible to suffer ill effects. "Mushroom poisoning" can be caused by:

- Eating a toxic mushroom

- Eating a rotten mushroom

- An allergy or sensitivity to a particular mushroom (very common)

- Eating too much mushroom in one meal

- Eating *Coprinus atramentarius* with alcohol

- Regional or substrate-related chemical variations, possibly due to different species that cannot be differentiated macroscopically, or due to a mushroom's propensity for accumulating minerals.

When trying a new species of mushroom for the first few times, be sure to try only a small amount. Mushrooms are a different kingdom than animals and plants, and have some unusual proteins that many people find difficult to digest. They often cause odiferous gas, and sometimes a heavy feeling in the stomach.

Mushrooms are more easily digested cooked than raw, as cooking helps to break down some of the proteins. If you are trying a mushroom raw for the first time, even if you have eaten this mushroom cooked, try only a small amount. We do not recommend eating large amounts of mushrooms raw. We have a few recipes that include raw mushrooms, but just in small quantities. Cooking also breaks down the chitin that mushrooms have in their cell walls, making the nutrients in them more digestible. Some types of mushroom are also rendered more digestible or more palatable by par-boiling and throwing out the water.

If you are serving wild mushrooms to others, please let them know what you are serving, as wild mushroom allergies are common. If you take mushrooms to a potluck, please label them prominently. We know a number of people allergic to such commonly eaten mushrooms as boletes, chanterelles and hedgehogs. Alison is allergic to *Russula olivaceous*, although she can eat *Russula xerampolina*, *R. brevipes* and *R. cyanoxantha*. She's also allergic to *Chroogomphus* spp.

Given all these negatives, why should you eat wild mushrooms? Many are delicious and delectable. They vary in flavor as much as the differences between lettuce, carrots and asparagus; or between apples, oranges and bananas. Many mushrooms lend a savory quality to dishes, which the Japanese refer to as umami; they make everything taste better. Some will flavor a dish with their own distinctive flavor; some have a more delicate flavor that blends well with other flavors; some absorb and carry the flavor of marinades, broths or sauces.

They are also very nutritious. Mushrooms are high in proteins and minerals, and low in fats, carbohydrates and calories. Mushrooms are much more efficient than plants at absorbing minerals (and water) from the soil. Many species of mushrooms have symbiotic relationships with plants, where the mushroom mycelium mines the soil for water and minerals, passing the extra on to the plant, while the plant supplies the fungus with extra carbohydrates from photosynthesis. Most of these species of mushroom cannot survive without their plant hosts, and most of the plant hosts cannot prosper or survive the rigors of the wild without their fungi.

If harvested properly and not to excess, wild-crafting mushrooms does not harm the environment, as they are the fruiting body of a perennial organism, equivalent to "an apple on a tree". When picking mushrooms, do not excessively disturb the duff around the area where they grow, so as not to disturb the mycelium. Carry a knife and brush to clean off dirt and debris in the field—during this process you may spread spores through your actions. If you cut off bits of mushroom, bury them under loose leaves or needles, so mycelial strands may continue to grow. Do not pick all specimens in an area, leave some to mature and spread their spores.

Please read the chapter "The Mushrooms," located before the recipes. It gives alternate common and scientific names for all the mushrooms in this book. With mushroom nomenclature in flux, the scientific names are changing. We have attempted to include the latest nomenclature. Many mushrooms have more than one common name, and we usually (but not always) use one of the common names in the recipes. If the different names are confusing, refer to this section, or the index.

The Mushroom section describes the best uses for different mushrooms and mentions procedures useful in their preparation. It covers the best methods of preservation for different species.

About the authors

ALISON GARDNER was born in Santa Barbara, California, and moved north to the Mendocino coast with her family in 1969, at the age of 10. She learned her first mushrooms the next fall, from an "old-timer", and has been an avid mushroom hunter and eater ever since. She has attended and teacher-aided for the local community college mushroom classes, as well as leading private mushroom tours.

She started cooking meals regularly for the family at age 13, learning from her mother, a cousin and a neighbor. She took a commercial cooking class in high school, and worked in two restaurants in her teens and early twenties. She has done some catering for weddings. She is also a botanist and potter, and still resides on the Mendocino coast.

MERRY WINSLOW:

When I first moved onto this land in Mendocino I found signs tacked to the trees: "No Mushroom Hunting! Violators will be prosecuted after our dogs are through with them!" I found the signs disturbing because of the hostility they projected, so I took them down. I was inspired, though, by the good foraging that the signs promised. For the first few years I lived here, I sought the wild edibles. I took many walks looking for mushrooms but never finding any I could recognize.

Finally I took Teresa Sholars' "Mushrooms of the North Coast" identification course at College of the Redwoods, and suddenly, I was SEEING mushrooms everywhere! Since then, I have found great quantities of edible mushrooms within a few miles of home. During that fateful class at C/R, I met Alison, who was the teacher's aide. Every week she would bring delicious dishes to class, which she had made with wild mushrooms. I convinced her that her artistry deserved a cookbook. Hence this partnership was born, and she has provided us with so many excellent tasting experiences since then that writing this cookbook has been a culinary adventure of the finest sort.

My own delight at foraging for the family began as a kid when I fished and dug clams on the shores of the Long Island Sound in New York. In suburbia, the only wild edibles I knew of were honeysuckle, crab apples, and onion grass, none of which I enjoyed eating. I was a frustrated hunter-gatherer until I learned the mushrooms, and since then, foraging in this mixed coniferous coastal forest has given me many hours of great pleasure and many fine meals. I'm so happy to be able to share the bounty with you!

Acknowledgments

I WOULD LIKE TO acknowledge my mother, Lois Gardner, for encouraging me to help in the kitchen and teaching me basic cooking. I would also like to thank my cousin, Sandra Wright, for encouragement and broadening my cooking skills. My other cooking mentors and teachers were Astra Thor, Cynthia Frank and Paul Katzeff. I would like to acknowledge Norman Shandel, Sr., for teaching me my first mushrooms as a child, and Teresa Sholars for expanding my mushroom repertoire. I would like to thank David Arora for writing *Mushrooms Demystified*, without which west coast mushrooms would still be a mystery. I would also like to acknowledge Ryane Snow for his encouragement and enthusiasm.
—*Alison*

I APPRECIATE MY PARENTS who let me run free in the forest behind our house in Rye, New York in the 1950's. My walks in the winter woods in search of mushrooms rekindle that joy and the timelessness of childhood. If not for Teresa Sholars, I wouldn't be able to tell a mushroom from a toadstool; she has opened my world beyond description. Most especially, my love and thanks go to my daughter Teddy, for supporting me in every project and always believing in me.
—*Merry*

WE ALSO WISH TO thank those who helped us bring this book to publication: the excellent cooks who have shared their recipes, Cypress House Publishing, The West Company, Pat Ferrero, Marshall Brown and the late Ryane Snow.

The Mushrooms

Agaricus

Agaricus is one of the most difficult of the mushroom genera to identify to species without chemical testing. This genus contains both edible and toxic species, some of which are very difficult to tell apart. More people are poisoned by agaricus than by any other type of mushroom. Be absolutely certain that you have correctly identified the species before eating the mushroom—they won't kill you but you might wish they had.

I (Alison) used to have trouble detecting the smell of phenol which is the toxin in the poisonous species of *Agaricus*. I picked what I thought were nice big juicy meadow mushrooms, cooked them and ate them. They were, instead, the toxic *Agaricus californicus*, and I threw up for about 3 hours. Ever since that time, I've had a nose that is very sensitive to phenol. If you can learn the smell of phenol the easy way, I'd recommend it over the hard way. If you cannot learn the smell of phenol, I would discourage you from eating wild agaricus. Crushing the base of the stalk will usually release the strongest phenol odor in the toxic species of *Agaricus*.

Edible species of *Agaricus* come in two distinct flavors: sweet and almondy, or classically mushroomy. The almond flavored ones such as *A. augustus* (the prince) are more subtle and in order to take advantage of their delicate flavor they should not be used in recipes where they will be overpowered. They are at their best in creamy dishes, or with potatoes, grains or pasta. They are also excellent in French onion soup and stir-fries. They can also be used in desserts. The horse mushrooms are intermediate in flavor, with a musty almondy flavor, and are good in almost any savory dish, including those with tomato-based sauces.

Some edible species of *Agaricus* found on the Mendocino coast include the prince (*Agaricus augustus*), the wine agaric (*A. subrutilescens*), the bleeding agaric (*A. fuscofibrillosus*), Smith's agaric (*A. smithii*), the horse mushroom (*A. arvensis*), the giant horse mushroom (*A. osecanus*), the crocodile agaric (*A. crocodilanus*) and the meadow mushroom (*A. campestris*).

All species of *Agaricus* can be preserved by freezing, drying, pickling or pressure canning.

Anise Clitocybes

There are several species of mushroom known of as anise clitocybes: *Clitocybe odorata* var. *pacificus*, *C. deceptiva*, *C. suaveolens*, and *C. fragrans*. They are small and often overlooked. Some years, there are very good fruitings of these delicacies. They have a powerful anise or fennel-like flavor (and odor) for such a small mushroom. They are excellent in puddings and custards, added to protein drinks, smoothies or milkshakes, combined with mint or spices for tea, made into a liqueur, or (in larger amounts) used with sausage or vegetables, or anywhere where you want a fennel flavor. They are best preserved through drying, or as a syrup.

Make sure you are sure of the identification—smell is key here, as there are some clitocybes that are quite poisonous.

Beefsteak Mushrooms

The beefsteak mushroom, (*Fistulina hepatica*) is a unique and unusual mushroom in cooking. It has the look of a nicely marbled steak, but its flavor is acidic and its texture somewhat slimy. It is quite good if you expect this, and work with it, but discovering this unexpectedly often turns people off. The beefsteak mushroom makes good "jerky" if marinated and dried. It's also good in sweet and sour dishes, dishes with lemon or other citrus, yogurt or sour cream, and curries. It may be preserved through drying or as jerky, or cooked and frozen.

Black Trumpets

Craterellus cornucopioides, horn of plenty, black chanterelle, black trumpets, or just "blacks" are welcome harbingers of the end of winter. Arriving in mid-winter to early spring, after many earlier mushrooms have waned, they provide us the opportunity to forage once more in our local forests and sweeten the inevitable cessation of mushroom season. Tasty additions to many recipes, black trumpets have a distinctive earthy flavor all their own and their colorful appearance in most dishes is a great asset. They are very versatile and can be substituted for chanterelles, hedgehogs or yellow feet or any of the milder-flavored mushrooms.

Blacks should be torn open to clean them before cooking or preserving, as their hollow stems collect fir needles and bugs. They may be rinsed in water, as their thin flesh does not easily water-log. Black trumpets are easily preserved by drying, and they reconstitute well. They may also be frozen either raw or cooked. Allow their sur-face to dry, if you wash them, before freezing them raw, and you can freeze them in bulk, as you will be able to pick a handful of frozen mushrooms out of the bag, and put the rest back in the freezer.

Blewits

It's always fun to eat purple food and blewits (*Clitocybe nuda* or *Lepista nuda*) are no exception. They have a mild flavor with a hint of citrus. They are excellent sautéed on their own, or used in many mild flavored dishes—soups, quiches, risottos, or with eggs or potatoes. If there has been a lot of rain, blewits often become water-logged. In this case, dry-sautéing them (without oil in the pan, releasing and evaporating the water out of them) before using them in a recipe can be appropriate.
Blewits may be frozen, dried, pickled or pressure canned for later use.

Blewits can be confused with the several species of poisonous lavender cortinarius if you are not familiar with them. For this reason, we would not recommend them for beginners. They are most easily differentiated from the cortinarius by spore color.

Boletes (Boletaceae)

Be careful if you have not eaten boletes before, as quite a few people are allergic to them. They are popular mushrooms with excellent flavor, and a prize to find, but we would recommend limiting a first tasting of any species to a small portion, then waiting a day or two to be sure you do not have an allergic reaction or intolerance before indulging further.

Boletes include, within the genus *Boletus*, the universally prized *Boletus edulis* var. *grandedulis* (formerly *B. edulis*, common names: king bolete, cep, porcini, gam-boni), *B. reginus* (formerly *B. aureus*, queen bolete), *B. mirabilis* (admirable bolete), *B. appendiculatus*, *B. abieticola* and *B. regius* (butter boletes), and the not-so-prized but edible *B. zelleri* (Zeller's bolete) and *B. chrysenteron* (cracked-cap bolete). Most of the bolete recipes in this book focus on the king bolete, as it is the most well-known and widely gathered of these species. The queen can be substituted in any of these reci-pes; it has a similar flavor and texture. *B. mirabilis* has a hint of citrus (without the sourness) to its flavor, and we have developed several recipes to which it is suited, but it is not limited to those recipes. The butter bolete has a more delicate nutty fla-vor and firmer texture; it is a pleasure to eat it just sautéed in butter, but it could be used in any savory recipe. *B. zelleri* and *B. chrysenteron* have a stronger and coarser flavor than the others. They are best used in chili, meatloaf, curries, or other dishes where a mushroom with a delicate flavor would not be tasted.

Leccinum manzanitae (Manzanita bolete) can also be used in most of the recipes for *Boletus edulis* in this book. Unlike other boletes, it rarely gets maggots. However, some people who can eat other boletes have an intolerance to leccinums, or possibly to a certain species of leccinum, so, again, if you have not eaten leccinums before, or if you are gathering them in a different region than usual, we recommend small portions to ascertain whether you may have an adverse reaction before chowing down on their abundance.

When cooking leccinums, like most boletes they tend to be soft and get slimy (cooked) as they age. We advise using only the button to half-open stage for cooking fresh; any larger are better dried (This advice holds for all boletes). The leccinum's tendency to turn black when sautéed can be averted by parboiling—heat water to boiling, add ½ teaspoon of salt per quart, slice or chop the mushroom and throw it into the boiling water for a minute or two, then drain and sauté, or cook as directed in the recipe.

Suillus (Slippery Jacks) are also included in the bolete family, and though they are sought-after in some countries, they are mostly neglected here, as there are so many other bigger, less slimy mushrooms to gather. Most species of *Suillus* are quite slimy when cooked fresh, and make an excellent facsimile of fried banana slugs. They are frequently used for soups, or are salted or pickled in some countries. They are sometimes cooked with rice or buckwheat. Peeling the cap helps. Also, they are not as slimy after drying, and in years of deficit can be dried and used to stretch the king bolete. There are only a couple species of *Suillus* that are mildly toxic, but of the edible ones, the best flavored are *Suillus brevipes* and *S. granulatus*; *S. lakei* and *S. ponderosus* are not bad, either, and are less slimy than the previous species. I have found *Suillus caerulescens* to have a rather unpleasant flavor, and have not bothered to try the other *Suillus* species of ill repute.

A confluence of environmental factors initiates the annual sprouting of the majestic *Boletus edulis*. Old timers say that the porcini will come up 10 days after the first good rain. After that first soaking rain, if the temperatures drop, and nature smiles, one may find these sturdy sentinels popping up in great profusion. The size and bulk of the boletes provoke great delight, for they are satisfying to cook and even better dried. If more rains and cool weather follow the initial rain, successive flushes of gambonis may be expected throughout the fall. In a year when the first rain is followed by a long dry spell, the harvest may be brief, and the secondary flushes may not happen.

Porcini (and most other boletes) are maggot magnets! It's a race to see who finds the mushroom first—the worms or you. Black fungus gnats lay their eggs in the soil and the little white maggots will burrow up inside the stem, which looks pristine from the outside. A wonderful large specimen may be riddled with worms while appearing whole, even in the button state. Then there are the deer, which can eat your whole crop overnight, leaving the bases with their tooth-marks. Boletes are also sought out by the banana slugs, millipedes, etc.

Everyone competes for these delectibles.

Candy Caps

There is no other mushroom like candy caps (*Lactarius fragilis* or *L. rubidus*). They are dessert mushrooms. They have a flavor similar to maple syrup, only without the sweetness. The candy cap is used to flavor desserts as well as entrees and its aroma can scent a closet for years, should you forget one in your coat pocket, as I did (Merry).

Candy caps can be difficult to learn to identify, as there are other species of *Lactarius* that look very similar and are mildly toxic. Be sure that you know the mushroom well before gathering it yourself. When fresh, candy caps do not have the same distinctive odor, as the distinguishing characteristic smell is not clearly revealed until the mushroom dries, making positive identification in the field somewhat tricky for novices. They do have an odor, but much milder, and often with a hint of curry. Not only are there toxic look-alikes in *Lactarius*, but a beginner could even confuse the deadly *Galerina* for a candy cap, so be sure of your identification.

The flavor of this mushroom is elicited by using a touch of sweetness so the recipes we offer are on the sweet side: desserts, fruit dishes, yams, winter squash, curries, baked beans and mashed potatoes.

When cooking candy caps, it is best not to fry them at a high temperature, as the flavor is somewhat volatile, and can lessen with high heat. Boiling or baking will preserve the flavor better.

Candy caps are usually preserved by drying. If you dry them, be sure to use a low heat source, such as a dehydrator which can be set for 85 to 90° F. They often will lose flavor if they are dried in an oven or at a high temperature. Stored in air-tight jars in a cool dark place, candy caps will keep for years, ready to add their distinctive flavor to future culinary adventures.

Candy caps can also be preserved by making them into syrup. The syrup will store for several months in the refrigerator, or may be canned for long-term storage. They can also be used to flavor alcohol (brandy, rum, vodka, whiskey), which can then be used straight, in mixed drinks, or to flavor foods.

Cauliflower Mushrooms

Sparassis crispa, also known as *S. radicata*, or the cauliflower mushroom, resembles a large cauliflower, brain, or pile of pasta. It is best treated like pasta, or used in casseroles or stir-fries after par-boiling. It is sometimes bitter if it is not par-boiled. It may be cooked and frozen for later use.

Chanterelles

Often the first golden chanterelles (*Cantharellus formosus*, formerly *C. cibarius*) appear in the late summer, if we get a little rain or drippy fog, and will continue until hard frosts. They can sometimes be found late into the winter in protected spots in the forest. The white chanterelle (*C. subalbidus*, formerly *C. sibericus*) comes up a little later than the golden, as the weather cools. Thus chanterelles provide a lot of fresh food over the course of the year, which is good because they are among the least impressive of all mushroom species when dried and reconstituted. Many people have success cooking and freezing chanterelles in small portions for use out of season, and this technique can help prolong the enjoyment of these abundant fungi.

Chanterelles vary considerably in moisture content throughout the season. Early chanterelles (and store-bought ones) are often dry. Some recipes call for dry-sautéing chanterelles (without any oil), but if your chanterelles are dry ones, you may need to use a little oil or butter in these recipes. Many chanterelle recipes will say to sauté the mushrooms until they exude their moisture. If your chanterelles are dry, they may not do this, so use your judgment on when they're done enough. They should be cooked through, but not browned, for an equivalent.

On the other hand, if the weather has been really wet, the chanterelles may be water-logged, in which case, dry-sautéing them before using them in a recipe may be appropriate, if similar instructions are not already included. To dry-sauté, put the mushrooms in a dry frying pan over medium-high heat, and stir them until they exude their water and the water has evaporated.

Cantharellus formosus and *C. subalbidus* are the two species most commonly found in our area, and they are generally interchangeable in cooking. The other species of chanterelle, such as *C. cibarius*, *C. californicus* and *C. cascadensis* are interchangeable in recipes with these two, and chanterelles and hedgehogs interchange well in recipes. Chanterelles break into lovely curly pieces when you gently pull them apart, and prepared in this manner, emphasize the texture of the mushroom.

Trusty chanterelles will not disappoint you, once you find their habitat and patrol it regularly. You can leave the small ones to grow more and return to mark their progress until they are of sufficient size. Worms shun chanterelles, making them ideal keepers in the forest.

Chicken of the Woods

Chicken of the woods, also known as sulfur shelf (*Laetiporus conifericola, L. sulfureus,* or *Polyporus sufureus*), is not uncommon on the Mendocino coast, unlike hen of the woods, which has a similar name but does not grow here. Some people are sensitive to chicken of the woods, and find it difficult to digest, and the similar species, *Laetiporus gilbersonii*, which grows on eucalyptus, is particularly problematic, generally causing digestive upset. Par-boiling can improve the digestibility of *L. conifericola*.

Cocorras and Grisettes

We include some recipes for edible *Amanitas*, the cocorra: *Amanita calyptroderma* or *calyptrata*, and the grisettes: *Amanita vaginata*, *A. pachycholea* and *A. constricta*. These mushrooms have been used by local Italians for generations. Beginning mushroomers, however, should NEVER eat any *Amanitas*, as the toxic species can be lethal, and it is not worth the risk of a misidentification. Be one-hundred percent sure of your mushroom identification as a mistake can kill you.

Both the cocorra and the grisettes can have a fishy flavor to some people, particularly as the mushrooms get older, or if preserved by drying. The younger specimens are better for eating. Cocorras are frequently used by Italians in tomato sauces, and raw in salads. They are also good in chowders. Grisettes can be substituted for cocorras in any recipe. They can be dried or frozen to preserve them for later use, however, drying will increase the fishiness of their flavor.

Coral Mushrooms

The best coral mushrooms for cooking are the pink-tipped coral, (*Ramaria botrytis*) Always collect it when it is young, with pink tips, as when they age and turn tan, not only are they easy to confuse with toxic species of coral (which also age tan) but they become altogether flavorless. At its best, the pink-tipped coral mushroom does not have a lot of flavor, and, like its distant cousin, pig's ears, is better marinated, and corals may be substituted for pig's ears in recipes. The yellow coral (*R. rasilispora*), can be substituted in any recipe for the pink-tipped, however, it is easier to confuse with toxic species. The yellow coral can also be used, in small amounts (like 1 tea-spoon per serving) raw, in salads, for color, as can the red coral (*R. araiospora*). We do not, however, recommend using pig's ears raw in salads.

Coral mushrooms are best preserved as pickles, but may also be cooked and frozen.

Many people are sensitive to coral mushrooms and get diarrhea from them, so use caution in trying them out.

Cup Fungi

Orange peel fungus (*Aleuria aurantiaca)* is the only cup fungus commonly eaten and known to be edible. It may be added raw to salads to brighten them up and give a mushroom flavor.

Deer Mushrooms

The deer mushroom (*Pluteus cervinus*) is rarely found in abundance, but has a very long season. It is often found in the fall, but is almost as commonly found in the spring, late enough to be eaten with asparagus, which it compliments well. It has a kind of woodsy flavor reminiscent of leaf mold and fresh-cut grass. It is a good substitute for the straw mushroom, used in oriental cooking, to which it is related. Deer mushrooms may be cooked and frozen for later use, or pressure canned.

Flat-Topped Club Corals

There is one species of club coral worth eating, and it is excellent, with a sweet fla-vor. The flat-topped club coral (*Clavariadelphus truncatus*) is not common, but can be found occasionally. They are excellent sautéed in butter, if you only find a few. If you score a bunch, we have a couple of recipes to try. They are also good in potato dishes.

Ganodermas

The reishi mushroom (*Ganoderma lucidum*) does not grow wild here, but three other species of *Ganoderma* do. *Ganoderma oregonense* and *G. tsugae* are similar and have been found to have similar active components. *G. applanatum*, the artist's conk, reputedly has some of the same components, also. All species of *Ganoderma* may be added when making soup stock, or may be used for tea. It can be bitter if made too strong.

Ganodermas are preserved by drying, which they do easily.

Hawk Wing

The hawk wing (*Sarcodon* or *Hydnum imbricatum*) has a robust mushroom flavor, but can often be bitter, particularly with the older specimens. They can also be difficult to digest. Both these problems can be improved by par-boiling the sliced mushroom in salted water for 10 to 15 minutes, then draining. It may then be added to the recipe. Even with par-boiling, we would definitely recommend trying only a small amount the first time you eat it, as many people find it difficult to digest.

Hawk wings are best used in stronger-flavored dishes, such as red spaghetti sauce, or chilies, or marinated or pickled. Preserve them by pickling, or by par-boiling and freezing.

Hedgehogs

Hedgehogs (*Dentinum umbilicatum*, *Dentinum repandum*, *Hydnum umbilicatum*, *Hydnum repandum*) are among the most prolific of our winter mushrooms. Appearing in late fall, they are not susceptible to maggot infestation and thus may be harvested slowly. You may allow smaller ones to mature and return to your patches throughout the season to pick the larger ones. (Unless someone else finds them first!) They are also among the easiest for the beginning forager to identify. The underside, with its spiny teeth instead of gills, may be difficult to discern if you're far-sighted, but a hand lens will reveal from whence comes the genus name "Dentinum". Functionally they may be exchanged for chanterelles in most dishes, as their taste and texture are similar. Hedgehogs are best frozen for later use, but they may also be dried–they reconstitute better than chanterelles. They also make excellent pickles.

Jelly Fungi

Jelly fungi do not fare well with cooking. They can be used in salads, in small amounts, to brighten them up. The edible species include *Pseudohydnum gelatinosum,* or the toothed jelly fungus, which is the least slimy of the jelly fungi, and the unrelated *Leotia lubrica*, or jelly babies, and *L. viscosa*, or chicken lips. Unrelated to both of these genera are *Tremella mesenterica* and *Dacrymyces palmatus,* both called witches butter.

Lobster Mushrooms

The lobster mushroom, (*Hypomyces lactifluorum*), was rarely found on the Mendocino coast until recently. As a result, we have little experience with them. We have tapped a friend or two to present a few recipes for them, but we also suggest them as alternates in some recipes for other species. If we do a 2nd edition, it will probably include more recipes specifically for lobsters.

The lobster mushroom is unusual in that it is a parasitic fungus that grows on Russula brevipes, so you are eating two fungi at once.

Man on Horseback

Tricholoma flavovirens, (formerly *T. equestre*) is a very distinctive mushroom, very easy to identify, with lemon yellow gills and a yellow cap, shading to yellow/brown in the center. Some people, however, are allergic to it. It is a very delicious, mild flavored mushroom that is excellent as a key flavoring in bland dishes, such as potatoes, that will allow its rich subtle flavor to shine.

Man on horseback is best preserved by sautéing and freezing.

Matsutakes

Ahh! Matsutake! You can identify a matsutake (*Tricholoma magnivelare,* or *Armellaria ponderosa*) by odor alone. Venerated in Japan, for good reason, the matsutake lends its flavor well in many Japanese dishes. It also turns a basic chicken soup or French onion soup into a heavenly dish, is particularly good with chicken and enhances many other dishes, besides. It is sometimes used raw, in fine shavings, for flavoring; however it often will cause diarrhea if consumed raw in quantity.

Large, open matsutakes are often more tender and flavorful than the buttons, and though they sometimes get wormy or are eaten by rodents or deer, they are less prone to these problems than the boletes.

Matsutakes are best preserved by freezing, either plain or marinated, and sautéed.

Meadow Waxy Caps

The meadow waxy cap (*Camarophyllus pratensis*, or *Hygrophorus pratensis*) is similar to the chanterelle in appearance, but has neither its flavor nor texture. It is probably the best of Hygropheraceae for eating, however, it tends to be soft and watery, and has a very delicate flavor. It may be used to replace the deer mushroom, or in any mild-flavored recipes, where it won't be overpowered.

Milk Caps

Common edible milk caps on the Mendocino coast are the delicious milk cap (*Lactarius deliciosus*) with an orange exudate, and the bleeding milk cap (*L. sanguiifluus* or *L. rubrilactus*) with a maroon exudate, and the candy cap, which is treated separately. Milk caps have a mild, nutty flavor, though in some areas there are reports of some bitterness. However, they tend to have a grainy texture, which many people dislike. The young specimens of these species are of the best flavor and texture. Collect specimens in which the rims are still curled under, and which do not have the green staining which they get in age. Use the youngest specimens in recipes which call for sautéing or a short cooking, and use the older ones in soups or stews which will receive a long cooking.

Milk caps can be preserved by drying, freezing, pickling or salting.

Morels

Morels are not common on the Mendocino coast. Black morels (*Morchella elata*) are sometimes found the spring after a forest fire, and occasionally white or yellow morels (*M. deliciosa* or *M. esculenta*) may come up in imported wood chips or soil brought in for landscaping. We have included a few morel recipes, in case you're lucky and find some. Clean morels well, cutting them in half length-wise to check for bugs and debris inside. Morels must always be thoroughly cooked; they are toxic raw. Preserve them by drying.

Oyster Mushrooms

Oyster mushrooms (*Pleurotus ostreatus*) are beautiful, and very versatile. They are mild in flavor and are excellent sautéed in butter or oil, or used in stir-fries or cooked with potatoes or in risottos. They also make a good Alfredo sauce, for pasta. Best preserved by freezing.

Pig's Ears

A distinctive looking mushroom, the pig's ear (*Gomphus clavatus*) is easily identified by its purple ridges and stalk, and as easily camouflaged by its beige and brown cap. This mushroom has quite a good flavor when it is very young, but as it ages, it becomes flavorless and insipid. However, pig's ears retain a nice firm texture, and the older mushrooms take on and hold other flavors well. Pig's ears lend themselves well to smoking or marinating, delivering an improvement in flavor and contributing unique qualities to our recipes which follow. Smoked or marinated pig's ears are best used fresh, or frozen (cook marinated ones first), but can also be dried. Dried pig's ears remain tough when reconstituted, so should be ground into a powder for flavoring, or used in a soup or stew, where they will receive a long boiling.

Puffballs

Puffballs, including species of *Lycoperdon*, *Bovista* and the giant puffball, *Calvatia*, are found on the Mendocino coast, but not often in quantity. The giant puffballs are much more common inland. We are lacking in much experience with them, but they may be used like tofu or eggplant. There are not recipes in this book focused on them, but they may be used as alternate ingredients in a few recipes.

Russulas

The shrimp russula (*Russula xerampolina*) is the most commonly eaten of the russulas. It is actually a mild-flavored mushroom, and should not be eaten when it is so old that it is strong-smelling. It is one of the best of the russulas, along with the variegated russula (*R. cyanoxantha*). Both mushrooms have a mild flavor and a nice texture. The short-stemmed russula (*R. brevipes*) is also edible, if you can beat the rodents and slugs, and has a mild, almost nutty flavor, but has a somewhat granular texture, like the milk caps. All the russulas are good in soups and chowders, and can be frozen, pickled or salted to preserve them. Drying toughens their texture, and shrimp russulas get strong-flavored from drying.

Shaggy Manes

The shaggy mane (*Coprinus comatus*) is a delicious mushroom with a mild, nutty flavor and a good texture. It is excellent sautéed on its own, or with eggs. It is well-suited to putting in chowders, quiches or on pasta with an alfredo sauce or a pesto. They are also excellent stir-fried with vegetables. Shaggy manes, must, of course, be used the same day as you pick them. Stored in your refrigerator, they will turn to ink overnight. After cooking, they will keep a few days in the refrigerator, or may be frozen for later use. They may be cooked and frozen, or pickled, but may not be dried.

Sweetbread Mushrooms

The sweetbread mushroom or spy mushroom (*Clitopilus prunulus*) is a small, nondescript pink-spored mushroom, which can easily be mistaken for several toxic mushrooms, and is recommended only for experienced mushroomers who are familiar with it. It has a distinctive odor, and a robust mushroom flavor, and is excellent in gravies, potatoes, pastas and many other dishes. It is rarely found in excess, but can be either dried, or cooked and frozen for later use.

Turkey Tails

The turkey tail mushroom (*Trametes versicolor* or *Coriolus versicolor*) is used medicinally in the orient. It may be used as an ingredient in broth or stock, or may be made into a tea or an alcohol extract. Dry to preserve for later use.

Volvariella

Like the deer mushroom, which is in the same family, the common volvariella (*Volvariella speciosa*) has a grassy flavor. It is closely related to the oriental straw mushroom. It can easily be mistaken for an *Amanita* when it's young and the gills are still white, but their pinkish-tan spore print is a give-away. Preserve by freezing, pickling or pressure canning.

Yellow Foot or Winter Chanterelles

The yellow foot, winter chanterelle, or funnel chanterelle (*Craterellus neotubaeformis* or formerly *Cantherellus infundibuliformis*), is slight and thin fleshed. Its flavor is somewhat musty, which some people really like and others do not particularly care for. It is a mushroom that many would overlook or not bother with if it were not for the fact that this mushroom is often out when not much else is—December until the weather warms—often through April.

Like the black trumpet, winter chanterelles have a hollow stem, and should be torn in half to check for debris and bugs in the stalk.

The flavor of this mushroom pairs well with beer, sausages, sharp cheddar, sauerkraut and green olives. It is also a good choice for strong-flavored dishes like curries and chilies.

Winter chanterelles can be frozen raw for later use. Clean them before freezing, and allow the surface to dry. Freeze them spread on a cookie sheet or loosely placed in a bag so they don't stick together. After they are frozen, pack more tightly in bags. Their thin flesh allows you to chop them while still frozen and add them to the pot without defrosting them.

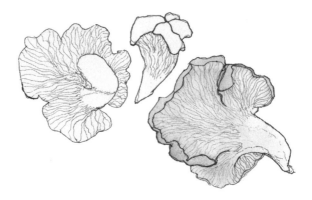

Breakfast Foods

Sunny Subrutilescens

This is a lovely way to enjoy the beauty of this tasty mushroom.

Serves 1

¼ to ½ cup spinach or kale, optional

1 fresh *Agaricus subrutilescens* cap

butter for sautéing

1 slice of bread

1 slice cheddar or jack cheese

1 egg per serving

1 large slice tomato

Steam or stir-fry the kale, if using. Set aside. Sauté the agaricus cap in butter on both sides until it is soft and cooked through. Meanwhile, toast the bread under the broiler on one side, flip, and melt cheese on it. Cook the egg sunny-side up, or flipped over, if you prefer. Assemble open faced onto the toasted bread: mushroom cap, greens, tomato, and top with the egg.

This may be made low-carb by omitting the bread and melting the cheese onto the mushroom. Sauté the gill side first, flip and sauté the other side, Just before it's done, place the cheese on top and lid the pan for a minute. Stack the remaining ingredients onto the mushroom cap and serve.

Smoky Scrambled Eggs

Serves 2

1 small smoked pig's ear (about ¼ cup chopped—see page 255)

2 teaspoons oil or butter

1 chanterelle, chopped

½ red bell pepper (optional)

¼ cup sausage or chopped ham (optional)

4 eggs

2 tablespoons grated cheddar cheese

Sauté mushrooms, pepper, and sausage in the oil or butter over medium heat. When done, add eggs and cheese, and scramble until done.

Italian Omelet

This can also be made with the cocorra or grisette.

Serves 1

½ cup chopped *Boletus*, *Leccinum*, or *Suillus* sp.

2 tablespoons chopped onion

Olive oil, for sautéing

1 clove garlic, minced

Pinch of Italian seasoning (oregano, rosemary, thyme, and/or sage)

1 slice mozzarella cheese

¼ cup spaghetti sauce

2 eggs

2 teaspoons milk or water

1 teaspoon Parmesan cheese

Sauté the onion and mushroom in olive oil. Add minced garlic and Italian seasoning when the onions and mushrooms are done and sauté a minute more. Break eggs into a small bowl, adding milk or water. Whip slightly with a fork. Oil and heat a small frying pan or omelet pan, over medium heat, and add the eggs. Turn down to low heat. Place a slice of mozzarella cheese on half of the eggs, top with mushroom and onion mixture, and spaghetti sauce. Cover and cook over low heat until eggs are done and filling is hot. Fold over and serve with a sprinkle of Parmesan cheese.

Matsutake Omelet

For a quicker breakfast, marinate the mushrooms the night before.

Serves 1

½ cup sliced fresh matsutake

⅓ cup chopped onion

1 tablespoon soy sauce

1 tablespoon sweet white wine, sherry, or mirin (Japanese rice cooking wine)

¼ cup chicken broth

1 teaspoon butter

2 eggs

2 teaspoons milk

1 slice jack cheese (garlic jack is good)

1 tablespoon sour cream

Toss the matsutake with soy and wine in a small saucepan. Allow to marinate ½ hour. Add onion and broth and simmer gently until broth has just evaporated (this part can be done the night before, in which case, just re-heat the mushrooms in the morning). Melt the butter in a small frying pan or omelet pan over medium heat. Stir together the eggs and milk; pour into the frying pan; turn down to low. Top with a slice of cheese and the mushroom mixture. Cover and cook over low heat until set. Top with sour cream, fold over, and serve.

Triple Smoked Omelet

Serves 2

2 slices bacon, chopped

½ cup sliced smoked pig's ears (recipe page 255)

¼ cup grated smoked Gouda

¼ cup chopped onion

¼ cup thinly sliced red bell pepper

3 to 4 eggs

1 tablespoon milk or water

1 tablespoon butter or oil

In a small frying pan, cook the bacon over medium heat until it is done. Drain the bacon on paper towels; pour off excess grease. In the same pan, sauté the onion and the pig's ears. When they are done, remove the pan from the heat. Add the bacon and red pepper and cover to keep warm.

Crack the eggs into a bowl, and whisk in the milk. Heat the butter or oil in a 9 to 10-inch cast-iron or non-stick frying pan. Pour in the eggs, lower heat. Sprinkle the cheese onto one half of the omelet, then add the filling mixture. Cover and cook over low heat until eggs are set. Fold in half, cut in half, and serve.

Mushroom Apple Sausage Scramble

Recipe by Craig Hathaway

Serves 2

½ pound sausage (bulk pork, or sliced chicken-apple)

1 apple chopped

½ cup zucchini, chopped or grated

½ cup *Boletus edulis*, chopped (or any other mushroom)

4 eggs

¼ cup grated cheddar cheese

2 tablespoons butter

Sauté sausage, apple, zucchini and mushroom in butter over medium heat until done. Add eggs and cheese. Cook, stirring with spatula, until eggs are done. Serve.

Mushroom Frittata

This is a base recipe, you may use different mushrooms or add other vegetables for a variety of flavors.

Serves 4

2 to 3 cups fresh mushrooms, chopped

½ onion, chopped

1 cup chopped fresh zucchini or lightly-steamed broccoli

4 cloves garlic

½ teaspoon rosemary, or thyme

2 tablespoons olive oil

8 eggs

½ teaspoon salt

½ cup ricotta or cottage cheese

½ cup cheddar or other cheese, grated

In an ovenproof 9 to 10-inch non-stick or seasoned cast-iron frying pan, sauté the onions, mushrooms and vegetables in 1 tablespoon of the olive oil over medium heat. Add the garlic and herbs when the mixture is nearly done. If using a cast-iron pan, try to keep the vegetables from sticking to the bottom.

Whisk the eggs with the salt in a bowl, and stir in the cottage cheese. Add the remaining tablespoon of oil to the vegetables and mushrooms in the pan and stir to coat the bottom of the pan with fresh oil. Turn on broiler to preheat. Add the eggs, turn down to low and cover for 5 to 10 minutes, until the bottom and sides are set, but the top is still runny. Sprinkle the grated cheese on top, and put under the broiler for a few minutes, until the top of the eggs is just set and the cheese melted. Remove from broiler, slice and serve.

Cheese and Winter Chanterelle Strata

A strata is like a savory bread pudding, often served for brunch, but good at any meal. This recipe can be started the night before, and baked the next morning.

Serves 12

4 cups winter chanterelles, torn

½ onion, chopped

2 tablespoons butter

½ to 1 loaf stale sourdough French bread

1½ cups grated Swiss cheese

1½ cups grated jack or cheddar cheese

6 eggs

2½ cups milk or half and half

¾ cup dry white wine or sherry

1 teaspoon thyme or tarragon

½ teaspoon salt

Sauté the mushrooms and onions in the butter, and set aside.

Dice or tear up the loaf of bread. Spread a layer of bread pieces over the bottom of a greased 9 by 13-inch glass baking pan. Mix the cheeses together, and sprinkle half of the mixture over the layer of bread. Spread the mushroom mixture over the cheese. Add another layer of bread, and top with the remaining cheese.

In a bowl, whisk the eggs. Then whisk in the milk, wine, thyme and salt. Pour the liquid over the strata. Cover with plastic or foil, and allow to sit in the refrigerator at least 4 hours, or overnight, so the moisture can equalize.

Remove the strata from the refrigerator a half-hour before baking, and preheat the oven to 325° F. Bake for 45 minutes to an hour, until golden brown on top, and set in the center.

Candy Cap Granola

Makes 5 ½ to 6½ cups

¼ cup oil or melted butter

2 tablespoons boiling water

3 tablespoons ground dried candy caps

½ cup honey

¼ cup brown sugar

2½ cups rolled oats

¼ cup freshly ground flaxseeds

¼ cup oat bran

¼ cup wheat germ

1 to 1½ cups chopped or whole nuts, seeds, coconut or a blend

1 teaspoon cinnamon

½ teaspoon cardamom

½ cup raisins

½ cup chopped dried apple

½ cup candied candy caps, (optional, see recipe on page 250)

Preheat the oven to 350° F. In a small saucepan, melt the butter. In a small bowl, pour the boiling water over the candy caps. When the butter is melted, add the honey and brown sugar, then add the soaked candy caps and bring it to a simmer. Turn off the heat, and put the pan in a warm place to keep the honey blend fluid.

Put oats and the nuts of your choice into a large bowl. Sprinkle with spices. Pour the contents of the saucepan over the oat mixture and stir. Lay the oat mixture out in a thin layer on a cookie sheet and bake in the oven, stirring every 5 minutes, until browned, about 20 to 30 minutes.

Remove from oven. Mix in the raisins, apples and coarsely chopped candied candy caps while the granola is still warm. Pack the granola flat against the pan with a spatula, to encourage clumping, and allow to cool completely. Break the clumps into bite-sized pieces and store in a moisture-proof container. Serve with milk or yogurt, over ice cream, or dry as a munchie.

Candy Cap Oatmeal

Old-fashioned rolled or steel-cut oats

3 or 4 candy caps per serving

Cook oatmeal using your favorite method, adding some fresh or dried chopped candy caps at the start of cooking. Best used with slow cooked oats, not instant. Serve with brown sugar, honey, or candy cap syrup (see recipe on page 219), butter, and milk, if desired.

Candy Cap Pancakes

Excellent with candy cap syrup (see recipe on page 219).

Serves 4

2 eggs, separated

3 tablespoons ground dried candy caps

1¼ cups milk

1½ cups flour

½ teaspoon salt

½ teaspoon baking soda

¼ cup yogurt or 1 teaspoon vinegar

Beat together the egg yolk, candy caps and milk in a mixing bowl. Allow to sit for 20 to 30 minutes for the mushrooms to soften. Stir in 1 cup of the flour.

In a separate bowl, beat the egg whites until they are stiff. Set aside. Preheat a griddle, over medium-high heat, with a little butter or oil for frying the cakes, until it is hot enough that a drop of water sizzles on it immediately.

Combine the remaining flour with the salt and soda, and stir it into the batter. Fold in the yogurt or vinegar and the egg whites, together.

Pour ¼ to ⅓ cup batter onto the hot griddle. When the edge is dry and the center begins to bubble, turn it to cook the other side. Cook until both sides are golden brown. If the sides don't brown enough, the pan is too cool; if the sides get too brown before the center cooks, the pan is too hot—turn the burner down a little. Continue to cook the cakes until the batter is used up. They may be served as they are cooked, or kept warm in a 250° oven while the rest are being cooked.

Candy Cap Waffles

These are excellent served with butter and candy cap syrup (see recipe on page 219).

Makes 6 waffles

1½ cup milk

3 eggs, separated

3 tablespoons ground dried candy caps

1½ cups flour

⅜ cup oil or melted butter

1 teaspoon vinegar

½ teaspoon salt

½ teaspoon baking soda

Beat together the milk, egg yolks and candy caps. Allow to sit for 20 to 30 minutes so the candy caps may soften. Stir in 1 cup of the flour, then the oil or butter. Preheat the waffle iron.

In a separate bowl, beat the egg whites and vinegar until the whites form stiff peaks.

Combine the remaining flour with the salt and soda, and stir it into the batter, then fold in the egg whites.

Grease the waffle iron unless it does not require it, and pour batter into the center until it nears the edges of the iron. Close the iron and cook until it registers done. Waffles may be served as they are baked, or may be kept warm in a 250° oven until all are ready. Leftover waffles may be frozen, and reheated in a toaster, later.

Candy Cap French Toast

Makes 4 to 5 slices

2 eggs

4 to 6 candy caps, fresh or dried

⅓ cup milk

4 to 5 slices of bread

Butter or oil for frying

Put the eggs, mushrooms and milk in a blender, and blend them until the mushroom is puréed. Pour the batter into a shallow bowl of sufficient diameter to dunk the bread slices.

Melt a teaspoon of butter in a skillet over moderate heat, and spread it over the bottom. When the pan is hot, dip a piece of bread in the batter, turning over to coat both sides. Put it in the pan and fry it until browned on the bottom, then flip and fry the other side. If you use a large pan, you may be able to do two slices at once. Continue until all the batter is used up.

Serve the toast with butter and maple or candy cap syrup (see recipe on page 219).

Mushroom Crepes

You may put dry powdered mushrooms in the crepe batter (candy cap for sweet crepes or porcini or other dried mushroom for savory), or leave it out and just use a mushroom filling. They may be served warm or cold, depending on the filling. You may want to prepare the filling first.

Makes 8 crepes

3 eggs

2 tablespoons flour

1 tablespoon dried mushroom powder (optional)

2 tablespoons milk or water

Butter for frying

Put all ingredients in a blender and blend. Heat a crepe pan or small frying pan on the stove, add about ½ teaspoon butter, and tilt and turn the pan to coat the bottom. Pour in about 2 tablespoons of the batter, and quickly tilt and turn the pan to spread it over the bottom. Cook about 1 minute, turn, and cook about 30 seconds on the other side. Stack up the crepes as they're cooked.

When all crepes are done, spread a line of filling from one side to the other, about ⅓ of the way from the side towards you. Roll the crepe away from you into a small log shape. Place on plates (2 is a common serving) and add a topping of your choice.

Fillings

Crepes may be filled with sweetened cream cheese, or the candy cap cream cheese filling used in candy cap cheese-filled dates (see recipe on page 34), or with candy cap whipped cream (see recipe on page 233). Both of these could be topped with candy cap syrup (see recipe on page 219).

For savory crepes, try filling them with sautéed mushrooms and topping with sour cream, or fill them with winter chanterelle spread (see recipe on page 38) and top them with paprika, or fill them with tapenade (see recipes on pages 35 to 36) or tapenade and cream cheese and top them with sour cream. Use your imagination!

Hot Milk Toast with Mushrooms and a Soft-Boiled Egg

This recipe is dedicated to my mother, Lois Gardner, who would make hot milk toast as a special breakfast on occasion when I was a child. She would often top it with a soft-boiled egg, and would, no doubt, have added the mushrooms had she thought of it.

—Alison

Serves 1
1 slice of bread
Butter
1 egg
1 cup milk
½ cup chopped mushrooms
Salt and pepper, to taste

Put water in a small saucepan to boil the egg. The water should cover the egg, but do not put the egg in, yet. Heat the water. Toast the bread, butter it, and put it in a wide, shallow bowl. Sauté the mushrooms in butter, if they are of a species that is tender. If they are too tough to eat sautéed, or if they are dried mushrooms, simmer them in a little water until they are tender. (Excess water may be saved to add to soup.) When the water for the egg is boiling, put the egg in for exactly 3 minutes. After the 3 minutes are up, drain off the water and refill the pan with cold water to cool the egg rapidly. Heat the milk in a sauce pan, stirring constantly, until it is comfortably hot, but not so hot as to form a skin.

To assemble, put the cooked mushrooms on the toast. Crack the shell at the wide end of the egg, peel the end and scoop the egg out with a spoon onto the mushrooms. Pour the hot milk over it, and serve immediately, seasoning to taste.

Appetizers, Dips, and Spreads

Dates in a Blanket

These may be baked or fried. If baking, preheat the oven to 450° F. The candy cap flavor does not stand out in this recipe, but blends nicely with the date and bacon flavors.

Makes 10 to 12

2 tablespoons ground dried candy caps

2 tablespoons boiling water

2 tablespoons minced almonds or pecans

2 tablespoons minced apple

10 to 12 large dates

4 or 5 slices bacon

1 teaspoon candy cap brandy (optional, see recipe on page 213)

Soak the powdered candy caps in the boiling water for 5 minutes to soften them. Toast the minced nuts in a dry frying pan if they are not already toasted. Stir together the mushrooms, nuts and apple. Add the brandy if using.

Slice the dates down one side, remove the pits and open the flesh well with your thumb. Stuff the dates with the filling. Cut the bacon slices in half and wrap a half slice around each stuffed date, securing with a toothpick. Fry in a covered frying pan, turning frequently to cook on all sides, or put on a cookie sheet and bake at 450° F for 15 to 20 minutes or until bacon is cooked and browned, turning as necessary. Serve warm or cold.

Candy Cap Cheese-Stuffed Dates

Inspired by Sophia Sutherland.

Makes 10 to 12

2 tablespoons ground dried candy caps

2 tablespoons boiling water

¼ cup cream cheese

2 teaspoons brown sugar, or more, to taste

pinch of mace or nutmeg

10 to 12 large dates

Pour the boiling water over the candy caps and allow to soften for 5 minutes. Meanwhile, slice the dates down one side and remove the pits. Open the cavity well with your thumb. Cream the cream cheese, and mash in the mushrooms, sugar and mace. Stuff into the dates, and serve.

Lobster Chips

Recipe by Anna Moore.
The same recipe works for boletes and gives a nice concentrated flavor. They can be used as a munchie, with a dip, or if made with boletes may be used in vegetarian stuffing in place of giblets.

Lobster mushrooms

Olive oil

Salt

Other seasonings as desired

Preheat the oven to 350° F. Slice mushrooms ¼ inch thick (lobsters should have firm white flesh inside). Drizzle with olive oil, season with salt and other seasonings (I like garlic pepper for a little zing), toss, and spread on an oiled baking sheet. Bake at 350° F for about an hour. The mushrooms will give off a lot of water and should be well vented. Stir several times during cooking (turn them if you can). You can taste them after about 45 minutes and continue cooking until they have a texture you like. The longer you cook them, the more crisp or jerky-like they will become but be careful not to burn them towards the end. They can be frozen at that stage and re-crisped in a toaster oven before eating. If you like them very crisp, you could remove them from the oven when they are well-roasted and finish them in a food dehydrator.

Chanterelle or Hedgehog Tapenade

Makes 3 to 4 cups

2 cups fresh hedgehog, black trumpet, yellow foot or chanterelle mushrooms

½ cup red onion, chopped

1 pimento pepper or ½ red bell pepper

½ cup pitted Kalamata olives

4 cloves garlic

1 tablespoon dried basil

3 anchovy filets (optional)

¾ cup butter

¾ cup olive oil

1 teaspoon thyme

¼ cup capers

Chop the mushrooms and sauté in a tablespoon of the butter until they release their water and the water has evaporated from the skillet. Sauté one minute more.

Put all ingredients into a food processor and process until minced and well mixed. Serve on pasta or spread on crackers, use as a sandwich spread, or serve on vegetables or meats. May be frozen in small batches for later use.

Porcini Tapenade

Makes about 2 cups
½ cup dried *Boletus edulis* or other dried bolete, packed
¼ cup red onion, chopped
½ cup olive oil
2 tablespoons capers
½ cup Kalamata olives (pitted)
2 cloves garlic
2 tablespoons sundried tomatoes, dried or oil packed
2 anchovy filets
½ cup butter
2 teaspoons dried basil
½ teaspoon dried rosemary
½ teaspoon dried oregano

Soak the mushrooms overnight in the olive oil. If using dried tomatoes, soak them with the mushrooms. To prepare the tapenade, run all the ingredients through a food processor until minced and blended. Serve on pasta, crackers, toast or use as sandwich spread, or serve on vegetables or meats.

Fig and Olive Tapenade with Candy Caps

This recipe was inspired by Andrea Luna.

Makes about a pint
1 cup dried black figs
½ cup fresh candy caps or ¼ cup dried
¾ cup Kalamata olives (pitted)
2 tablespoons capers
2 tablespoons olive oil
2 tablespoons lemon juice
1 tablespoon honey
½ teaspoon rosemary, minced

1 teaspoon thyme, minced

2 teaspoons whole grain sweet mustard such as Mendocino Mustard's "Seeds and Suds"

Put the figs and candy caps in a saucepan with ½ cup water, and bring to a boil. Put a lid on the pot and simmer for 5 minutes. Allow to cool. The figs should absorb most of the water.

Put the cooled fig mixture in a food processor and pulse until finely chopped but not smooth. Remove to bowl. Put the olives and capers in the food processor and chop, then add them to the figs. Mix in the oil, lemon juice, honey, herbs and mustard. Chill, and serve with crackers or bread.

Winter Chanterelle Cheese Spread

This is good spread on crackers for an hors d'oeuvre, or as a sandwich spread or crepe filling. May also be served as a cheese ball. The flavor of the winter chanterelles and the beer in this recipe go very well with sausages or liverwurst, and is also complimented by sauerkraut. Try it spread on a hot dog bun with a Polish sausage and sauerkraut!

Makes about 2½ cups

½ pound cream cheese

½ pound sharp or medium cheddar cheese

2 cups winter chanterelles

1 tablespoon olive oil

¼ cup dark beer (flat is fine)

½ teaspoon paprika

¼ teaspoon ground cumin

½ teaspoon salt

Sauté the mushrooms in the oil until they are soft. Cut the cheddar cheese into ½ inch dice, and process in a food processor. (If you don't have a processor, the cheese may be grated.) Add the cream cheese to the food processor a tablespoon at a time, then add the mushrooms and all other ingredients. May be scooped into a bowl and served immediately, or may be chilled overnight and rolled into a cheese ball and coated with chopped nuts or chives.

Roasted Garlic, Winter Chanterelle and Lentil Dip

This recipe can be made vegan.

> *Makes 3 ½ to 4 cups*
> 2 cups winter chanterelles
> ¼ cup chopped carrot
> 1 head of garlic
> ½ onion, chopped
> ¼ cup plus 1 tablespoon olive oil
> ½ teaspoon salt
> ¼ teaspoon thyme
> ¼ teaspoon rosemary (fresh if possible)
> 1 bay leaf
> ½ cup white wine
> 1½ cups broth (low salt chicken or vegetable) or water
> 2 tablespoons lemon juice
> 1 cup lentils (brown, green, or red)

Preheat the oven to 350° F. Toss the winter chanterelles, onion, 1 tablespoon olive oil and salt in a bowl. When well coated, spread out on a cookie sheet, with the head of garlic. Remove excess papery stem material from the top of the garlic. Roast in the oven until mushrooms and onion are well roasted and garlic is mushy. Mushrooms and onions will take 35 to 45 minutes and garlic 45 minutes to 1 hour, so transfer the mushrooms and onions to a bowl when they are done, and continue baking the garlic.

Meanwhile, put the lentils and carrots in a saucepan with the herbs. Add the broth or water. Cover and bring to a boil, then turn down to simmer. If using red lentils, add the wine after 10 minutes. If using brown or green whole lentils, add the wine after 20 minutes. Check occasionally and add a little bit more water if they get dry before they finish cooking. Red lentils will cook in 15 to 20 minutes, green in about 30 minutes, brown in about 40 to 45 minutes. When the lentils are done, allow them to cool. Remove the bay leaf.

Put lentils, onions, mushrooms, oil and lemon juice into a food processor. Squeeze garlic cloves out of their wrappers into the food processor. Process until smooth. If you don't have a food processor, mince the mushrooms and onions and mash everything together with a fork or a potato masher. Add salt as needed. (If using water, more salt will be needed than if broth is used.)

Boletus Butter

A savory spread that may be enjoyed on toast, crackers, sandwiches, vegetables or pasta. Also delicious on popcorn. You may substitute other species of Boletus, Leccinum, *or* Suillus, *or use dried smoked* Boletus *or pig's ears (directions for smoking are on page 255).*

Makes about ½ cup

2 tablespoons ground dried king bolete

½ cup butter, softened

1 clove garlic, minced or pressed

1 tablespoon fresh minced basil (or 1 teaspoon dried)

½ teaspoon fresh oregano

Cream the butter, then cream in all the other ingredients. The butter will keep two weeks in the refrigerator.

For a softer, lower cholesterol version, blend ¼ cup butter with ¼ cup olive oil in a food processor, then blend in other ingredients.

Black Trumpet Butter

Serve this on bread or crackers or use this flavored butter to cook your breakfast eggs, or put on cooked vegetables or popcorn.

½ cup minced fresh black trumpets or winter chanterelles

½ cup butter, softened

1 clove garlic, minced or pressed

2 tablespoons minced parsley, chervil, or tarragon (optional)

Sauté the mushrooms in one tablespoon of butter until they are well cooked.

Allow to cool slightly, then stir this mixture into the softened butter, along with the parsley and garlic. Keep refrigerated when not in use; will keep about 1 week.

For a softer, version, blend ¼ cup butter with ¼ cup olive oil in a food processor, then blend in other ingredients.

Horn of Plenty Sour Cream Dip

Makes about 3 cups

8 ounces cream cheese, softened

8 ounces sour cream

1 teaspoon butter

⅓ cup minced onions

1 cup minced horn of plenty mushrooms

2 cloves garlic, minced

Pinch of ground cloves

¼ teaspoon thyme

½ teaspoon salt

¼ cup minced red bell pepper

Cream the cream cheese, and mix in the sour cream.

Sauté the onions in the butter until they soften and begin to get translucent. Add the mushrooms and sauté until the water is cooked out of them and evaporated. Add the garlic, along with the thyme and the cloves. Sauté a few minutes more until the garlic becomes fragrant. Add this to the creamed mixture while still hot; this will smooth out any lumps in the cream cheese. Mix in the salt and minced red bell pepper. Serve with crackers, chips, or raw vegetables.

Mushroom Salami Bites

Serves 6 to 8

1 cup chopped mushrooms

1 teaspoon olive oil

4 oz. cream cheese, room temperature

1/2 pound package salami slices

Sauté the mushrooms in the olive oil. Blend them into the cream cheese while they are still hot. Put a heaping teaspoon of the cheese mixture on each salami slice and fold in half. Chill and serve.

Cocorra Dip

This is also good as a dressing for fish in place of tartar sauce. Grisettes may be substituted for the cocorra.

Makes about 3 cups

1½ cups finely chopped *Amanita calyptroderma*

½ cup finely chopped onion

1 tablespoon olive oil

3 cloves garlic, minced

½ teaspoon rosemary, minced

2 anchovy fillets, minced

2 tablespoons oil-packed sun-dried tomatoes

8 ounces cream cheese, room temperature

1 cup sour cream

¼ teaspoon grated lemon rind

2 tablespoons lemon juice

¼ teaspoon salt or to taste

Pinch of nutmeg or mace

Sauté the mushroom and onion in the oil until the mushroom is well-cooked and any water expelled from the mushroom has evaporated. Add the garlic and cook until fragrant. Remove from heat and put into a bowl. Add the rosemary, anchovies, tomatoes and cream cheese. Cream together until the cream cheese is smooth and it is well mixed. Stir in sour cream and remaining ingredients. Chill before serving.

Smoky Eggplant Dip

Makes 3 to 4 cups

1 small or one half of a large eggplant

¼ cup spaghetti sauce

¾ cup fresh smoked mushrooms (see recipe on page 255)

½ teaspoon salt, or to taste

2 cloves garlic

¼ cup sour cream

1 tablespoon olive oil

Wrap eggplant in foil and barbecue or bake until soft, (preferably a day ahead). Alternatively, you may roast the eggplant over the flame on the stove until the peel burns and the center is soft. Rotate the eggplant a few times during cooking. Try to keep the eggplant whole, while letting the skin char. The skin will crack and burn, and the juice will leak out on your stove but it's easy to clean up and the flavor of the eggplant when cooked this way is very delicious. Remove the soft, charred eggplant to a bowl to cool until it can be handled, and then gently peel off the burnt skin and discard, scraping the flesh off the inside if any sticks, and putting the eggplant in clean bowl.

Dice the cooled eggplant. In a non-cast-iron frying pan, over medium heat, sauté the eggplant and garlic in the olive oil for a few minutes, until the eggplant is mushy. Add spaghetti sauce and the smoked mushrooms. Cook until thick. Cool. Mash, or process in a food processor. Add sour cream and salt. Serve with chips, crackers, or raw vegetables.

Cheesy Eggplant Dip

Follow above recipe but stir in ½ cup grated cheddar, smoked Gouda, provolone or mozzarella cheese after cooking, but before cooling the dip.

Vegan Roasted Garlic-Hedgehog Sandwich Spread

This can also be used as an hors d'oeuvre spread for crackers or baguette slices. It may also be made with chanterelles. If you cannot find red lentils, you may use green or brown, but they will need to be cooked longer, and they have a stronger flavor.

Makes about 1 quart

1 head of garlic

4 cups minced hedgehog mushrooms

2 tablespoons olive oil

½ cup red lentils

1 teaspoon salt, or to taste

Preheat the oven to 350° F. Drizzle the olive oil on the mushrooms, and toss to coat. Spread them on a baking sheet, and put the garlic head (do not peel the garlic) on the sheet too. Cover with foil and bake for 1 hour. Remove them from the oven and allow to cool.

While the mushrooms are cooking, put the lentils in a saucepan with 1½ cups of water. Bring to a boil, turn down heat and cover, simmering for 20 to 30 minutes, until the lentils are soft and the water is absorbed. Remove from heat and allow to cool.

Put the lentils into a bowl and mash them. Pull the garlic head apart and squeeze the flesh of the cloves into the lentils. Stir in the mushrooms, salt to taste.

Matsutake Won Tons

Makes about 30

½ pound pork, ground or cut into chunks

2 cups matsutakes, chopped

1 tablespoon chopped fresh ginger root

3 cloves garlic

3 green onions, chopped

1 tablespoon rice vinegar

¼ cup chopped cilantro

¼ teaspoon crushed red pepper flakes

1 teaspoon sesame oil

1 tablespoon soy sauce

1 (12 ounce) package square wonton wrappers

2 quarts peanut oil for frying (optional)

Sriracha chili sauce

Combine the pork (if not already ground), matsutakes, ginger, garlic, green onion, vinegar, cilantro, crushed red pepper, sesame oil, and soy sauce in a food processor. Pulse until the mixture is finely minced. Transfer to a bowl. If the pork was pre-ground, mix it in now.

Separate the wonton wrappers and lay them out on a clean surface. Spoon 1 tablespoon of the pork mixture into the center of each wrapper. Moisten the edges of the wonton wrappers with water, fold over the filling to form a triangle, and press together to seal. Won tons may be fried, steamed, or cooked in soup (see recipe on page 90 for a Matsutake Won Ton Soup recipe).

To steam the won tons, cut pieces of parchment paper a bit larger than a won ton; put the won tons on the parchment pieces and put them into a steamer. Steam over hot water for 10 minutes. Serve with a dipping sauce made of ¼ cup soy sauce, 2 tablespoons rice vinegar, ¼ teaspoon toasted sesame oil and ½ teaspoon Sriracha.

If you are planning to fry the won tons, pour the peanut oil into a large pot and preheat to 365 degrees F (180 degrees C). Gently drop wontons into the hot oil and cook them until they are golden brown, about 5 minutes. Remove to paper towels to drain.

Admirable Baked Brie

Makes an 8-ounce round of Brie

1 teaspoon butter

2 cups *Boletus mirabilis*, finely chopped

Grated rind from 1 lemon

2 tablespoons lemon juice

1 tablespoon sugar

¼ cup water

¼ teaspoon cornstarch

An 8-ounce round of Brie cheese

Preheat the oven to 350° F. Sauté the mushrooms in the butter until soft in a non-reactive pan (not cast iron).

Mix together the water, sugar, lemon juice and rind, and the cornstarch, and add to the mushrooms. Bring to a boil, stirring constantly until it thickens slightly. Remove from heat.

Put the Brie in an ovenproof dish, smother with the lemon-mushroom sauce, and bake about 15 minutes, or until soft. Serve immediately with crackers or fresh crusty bread.

Wrapped Baked Brie with Candy Cap Syrup

Recipe from Donna French.

Makes an 8-ounce round

8 sheets of phyllo dough, thawed according to the directions on the package

1 8-ounce round of Brie cheese

⅔ cup butter

1 cup candy cap syrup (see recipe on page 219)

½ cup macadamia nuts

1 ripe pear, preferably Bosc or other firm variety

Preheat the oven to 350° F. Melt the butter.

Keeping the remaining phyllo dough sheets damp by covering with plastic or a barely damp dish towel, spread the first sheet out on a clean counter, and brush the top with butter. Stack on the next sheet, brushing the top with butter. Repeat with remaining sheets until all eight are stacked with butter in between each layer, and on the top surface. Place the Brie cheese in the center, and wrap the phyllo dough around it. Put it in a baking dish and bake for about 45 minutes or until it is golden brown.

Meanwhile, combine any remaining melted butter with the candy cap syrup, and when the cheese is nearly done baking, heat to a simmer. Chop the macadamia nuts. Slice the pear thinly, cross-wise with the core.

Remove the cheese from the oven, pour the syrup over it, and sprinkle with macadamia nuts. Serve with pear slices, a knife and a spoon. To eat, guests may slice a piece from the wrapped cheese and place it on a pear slice, then use the spoon to ladle the gooey center of the cheese, syrup, and macadamias over the slice. Be sure to provide napkins.

Chanterelle Stuffed Chilies

From Nikki Guerrero, Hot Mama Salsa Company. Use Joe Parker red peppers or other sweet red peppers—remove stems and seeds from peppers to prepare for stuffing.

Makes 10 to 12

1 cup chanterelles, chopped

1 tablespoon olive oil

1 cup white cheddar cheese, grated

¼ cup Parmesan cheese, grated

¼ cup herbed cream cheese

3 cloves of garlic, minced (about 2 teaspoons)

½ teaspoon chopped thyme

Salt and pepper to taste

10 to 12 Joe Parker or other mild red peppers

Preheat the oven to 400° F. In a bowl, toss the chanterelles and olive oil. Lay the chanterelles out on a sheet pan. Bake at 400° F for 20 minutes until the mushrooms give up their water. Add the garlic and roast for an additional 10 minutes.

Remove from the oven and turn down the heat to 350° F. Mix the mushrooms with the cheeses and herbs, salt and pepper, and stuff into the peppers. Roast in the oven for 30 minutes. Serve warm.

Cocorra Mousse Tapas

This mousse may be served as tapas or as a side dish with dinner or lunch. Prepare a 9 by 5-inch loaf pan by buttering the inside and then coating it with breadcrumbs. Fill a hot water bath in a larger pan that it will sit in, placed in the oven.

Serves 10 to 12

2 tablespoons olive oil

1 onion, coarsely chopped

3 cups coarsely chopped cocorra

1 red bell pepper, coarsely chopped

3 tomatoes, chopped

3 saffron stigmas

2 sprigs chervil or parsley, chopped

2 cloves garlic, chopped

½ cup white wine

7 eggs

½ cup cream

½ teaspoon salt

Preheat the oven to 225° F, with the water bath in the oven.

Sauté the onion and mushroom in a skillet until they are done and any water exuded from the mushroom has evaporated. Add the peppers, tomatoes, saffron, chervil and garlic and sauté until the garlic becomes fragrant.

Cool slightly, then put in a food processor and process until minced, but not pureed. Add wine, eggs, cream and salt and process until just mixed. Pour the batter into the prepared pan, cover with foil and bake in the water bath for 1 hour and 10 minutes. Cool, then chill. Loosen the sides with a knife, and jiggle the pan gently until the mousse is free. Invert onto a platter, slice and serve with the following sauce:

Sauce

1 cup mayonnaise

1 clove garlic, pressed

2 tablespoons minced green Spanish olives

Mix all ingredients together. Spoon a dollop onto each slice of mousse.

Candy Cap Glazed Nuts

Makes 2 cups

¼ cup candy cap syrup (see recipe on page 219)

2 cups unsalted nuts—peanuts, cashews, pecans, or almonds

Pinch of salt

Preheat the oven to 350° F. Toss the nuts in the syrup and salt.

Spread them out on a rimmed cookie sheet. Bake for about 15 minutes, stirring them and checking every 5 minutes, until nuts are browning and syrup is caramelized. Remove from the oven. Spread the nuts out on the cookie sheet to dry. They will stick together if they touch. If they remain sticky, finish in a food dehydrator or warm oven.

Dried Black Trumpet Veggie Dip

Makes about a quart

1 tablespoon butter

1 red onion, minced

2 cloves garlic, minced

¾ cup water

½ cup dried black trumpets

1 pint sour cream

1 cup finely grated raw zucchini or minced spinach

1 teaspoon salt, or to taste

Sauté onion in butter till transparent. Add garlic. Sauté a few minutes more.

Put mushrooms and water in blender, and blend on a low setting until chopped. Add both mushrooms and the blending water to the sautéed onion. Cook off excess water, until moist but not wet. Cool. Combine with the sour cream and other ingredients in a bowl, and serve with chips, crackers, or fresh raw vegetables.

Pickled and Marinated Mushrooms

Lemony Marinated Mushrooms

This recipe is reprinted from Gathered Mushroom Recipes, *a booklet by Teresa Sholars' fall 1981 mushroom class at the Fort Bragg branch of College of the Redwoods.*

Makes about a half-gallon

8 cups mushrooms, sliced if large ones

2 cups water

1 cup olive oil

Juice of 3 lemons

1 cup sliced celery

2 cloves garlic, crushed

1 slice fresh fennel or ½ teaspoon fennel seed

1 teaspoon chopped fresh chervil

1 small bay leaf

1 scant teaspoon coriander seed

10 peppercorns

¾ teaspoons salt

Put all ingredients into a large pot and bring to a boil. Simmer 6 to 10 minutes, stirring occasionally. May be hot-packed, or cool, put in jars and refrigerate.

Pickled Matsutake

This recipe is reprinted from Gathered Mushroom Recipes, *a booklet by Teresa Sholars' fall 1981 mushroom class at the Fort Bragg branch of College of the Redwoods.*

Makes about a quart

1 pound matsutakes

4 green onions, chopped

3 tablespoons sherry

3 tablespoons lemon juice

2 tablespoons sugar

1 tablespoon tamari

1 teaspoon salt

Preheat the broiler. Slice large caps ⅜-inch thick. Broil until brown.

Combine the remaining ingredients in a saucepan. Bring to a simmer, covered, over moderate heat and simmer for 5 minutes. Cool. Combine the mushrooms with the sauce, stirring to coat all pieces. Refrigerate at least one day before serving.

Marinated Matsutakes

These are excellent used in most matsutake recipes. The soy and sesame oil enhance the flavor of the mushroom.

Makes about 1 cup

About 1½ cups sliced matsutakes (one large or 3 to 6 buttons, depending on size)

¼ cup soy sauce

¼ cup sherry or mirin

½ teaspoon toasted sesame oil

1 tablespoon sesame seeds (optional)

Put the mushroom slices in a shallow container with a lid. Add the soy, wine, and sesame oil. Cover and allow to marinate in the refrigerator a minimum of

½ hour, and several hours or overnight is better. Stir mushrooms occasionally while marinating, flipping them to allow all sides of all pieces to come into contact with the marinade. Cook as directed in another recipe or, to serve as a side dish, simmer them in the marinade until the marinade reduces into a sauce. Garnish with sesame seeds.

Marinated Blewits

This is an interesting condiment to serve with pork, ham, chicken or fish.

Makes about 1 cup

1¼ cups blewits

¼ cup orange juice

1 tablespoon lemon juice or cider vinegar

1 tablespoon candy cap syrup (see recipe on page 219) or honey

2 teaspoon soy sauce

½ teaspoon lemon or orange rind

3 drops toasted sesame oil

Pinch of nutmeg or mace

Dry sauté the blewits until they release their juices and the water evaporates. Put all remaining ingredients into a bowl or container. Add the mushrooms and stir to coat. Cover and marinate in the refrigerator for several hours or overnight. They will keep for up to a week, refrigerated. They may be canned, but canning will change the flavor due to cooking the orange juice.

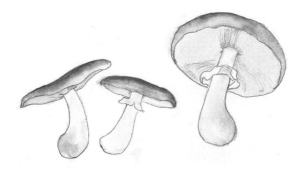

Marinated Boletus mirabilis

This makes a nice addition to a green salad, or a nice condiment to serve with fish or chicken.

Makes about 1 cup

1 cup sliced *Boletus mirabilis* buttons, or up to half-open mushrooms

2 tablespoon lemon juice

½ teaspoon grated lemon rind

2 tablespoon olive oil

¼ teaspoon thyme (lemon thyme if available)

pinch of nutmeg

pinch of salt

Dry sauté the mushrooms until they release their water and it evaporates. Put them into a bowl, add all other ingredients, tossing them to cover the mushrooms. Cover and refrigerate at least 3 hours, tossing occasionally. They will keep up to a week in the refrigerator.

Olive-Flavored Hedgehog Garnishes

These little garnishes may be used on individual hors d'oeuvres or may be used to garnish a martini in place of an olive. Small winter chanterelles may be used in place of hedgehogs

Makes about 1 cup

1 cup *Dentinum umbilicatum*, preferably 1 inch or smaller in cap size

the brine from a jar of green Spanish olives

Put the mushrooms in a small saucepan. Cover with the olive brine. Bring to a boil, cover and simmer 5 minutes; remove from heat and allow to cool. Store in the brine in the refrigerator until ready to use.

Pickled Mushrooms

This is a generic pickle which can be used with most mushrooms. It may be hot-packed in jars, or stored in the refrigerator. Adding a grape leaf to a jar of pickles helps keep them crisper.

Makes about 2 pints

4 cups mushrooms, whole if small or sliced or chopped if large

½ cup wine vinegar

½ cup water

1 teaspoon pickling spice

½ teaspoon salt

1 tablespoon sugar

4 cloves garlic, chopped

2 grape leaves (optional)

Put all ingredients into a saucepan, cover, and bring to a boil. Turn down and simmer for 15 minutes. May be hot-packed into sterile canning jars, putting a grape leaf in the bottom, then spooning in the mushrooms and filling to ½ inch from top with the boiling pickling liquid. If not canned, they will keep for several months in the refrigerator.

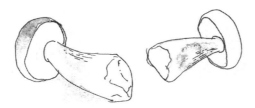

Pickled Chanterelles

Recipe by Dory Dan.

Makes 1 quart

4 cups chopped chanterelles

4 green onions

2 cloves garlic

¼ cup raisins

½ teaspoon salt

2 tablespoons olive oil

½ lemon (optional)

cider or white vinegar

Heat 6 cups of water to boiling in a large saucepan. Add the chanterelles and boil for 1 minute. Drain them in a colander, and rinse them under cold water. Put them into a bowl.

Chop the green onions and mince the garlic and sauté them together in a little of the olive oil. When done, stir them into the chanterelles, along with the remaining olive oil. Stir in the raisins. If using the lemon, cut off a ¼-inch slice, then cut the slice into quarters and stir them into the chanterelles. Squeeze the rest of the lemon over the mushrooms and discard the rest of the rind. Pack the mushrooms into a quart jar, and cover with white or cider vinegar. For a milder pickle, dilute the vinegar half and half with water. Either way, store in the refrigerator.

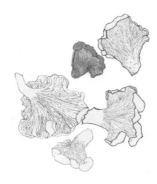

Fistulina Chutney

Makes 8 to 9 cups

2 cups *Fistulina hepatica*, chopped

5 cups cored and chopped apples

1 orange chopped with the skin on (organic recommended)

1½ cups raisins

1 onion, chopped

2 cups brown sugar

2 cups apple cider vinegar

1-inch piece fresh ginger

1 tablespoon cinnamon

½ teaspoon nutmeg

¼ teaspoon cayenne

1½ teaspoon salt

Mince or run through a food processor: the mushroom, apples, orange, onion and ginger. Put all ingredients into a large pot and simmer, covered, for ½ hour. May be hot packed and sealed in glass canning jars. Proportions of sugar, vinegar, and spices may be varied according to your taste.

Salted Mushrooms

Recipe by Irina Valioulina.

Irina uses the toxic peppery-flavored species of Lactarius: L. rufus, L. vineorufescens, L. chrysorheus, *and* L. scrobicularis, *in this recipe, with a soaking process to remove the toxins. This recipe may also be used with the edible* L. deliciosus *or* L. sanguifluus, *eliminating the soaking process, but not the par-boiling. It may also be used (without the soaking) with many other edible species, or a blend of mushrooms, or less desirable species such as* Russula brevipes *or* Suillus brevipes.

Makes about 2½ quarts
3 quarts mushrooms
Pickling or kosher salt
sliced garlic and black currant leaves, or dill

Soak the mushrooms in water for two days, changing the water twice a day. Then par-boil the mushrooms in water for 5 minutes.

In a gallon crock or jar, put a half-inch layer of salt on the bottom of the crock. Put a layer of mushrooms on the salt, caps down, put in a little garlic and a currant leaf or some dill and top with a ¼ inch layer of salt. Continue to layer mushrooms, herbs and salt, until all mushrooms are used. Finish with a layer of salt. If using a crock, top with the follower. If using a jar, you may fabricate a follower and use a light weight, or use skewers to hold the mushrooms down, bracing the skewers against the inside of the shoulder of the jar. Store the mushrooms in a cool place for 2 to 3 months. If all the species are edibles, they may be eaten after one week. If any of the toxics are included, they should salt for 6 weeks.

To eat the mushrooms, remove the mushrooms to be used, replacing the follower and weight on the remaining mushrooms. Soak the mushrooms to be used in water for ½ hour or more, and drain to remove the extra salt. Traditionally served with vodka. They are also good in a salad with lettuce, potatoes and onions.

Horn of Plenty Sauerkraut

Yellow feet may be substituted for the horn of plenty. Be cautious in using mushrooms in sauerkraut. Being high in protein, they might become toxic if the wrong bacteria got into the batch. Be sure the mushrooms are young and in good condition. If the kraut smells or looks rotten, gets moldy or gets pink or yellow discoloration, discard it.

Makes 1 quart

2 cups *Craterellus cornucopioides*, coarsely chopped

5 cups shredded cabbage

½ onion thinly sliced

2 cloves garlic, minced

1 tablespoon salt

Mix all ingredients in a large bowl. allow to sit for ½ hour.

Pack firmly into a wide mouth quart mason jar or small kraut crock, including the liquid that exudes from the cabbage. Fill to the top of the jar, packing firmly. Be sure cabbage is below the liquid level. Add a little water if necessary.

Screw on the lid and set the jar in a shallow bowl or on a plate and allow to ferment at room temperature for a few days to a week. Taste every day or so until sour to your liking. Some liquid may seep out under the lid; that is normal. An airtight seal is not necessary or desirable—this is an active, living food. When sour enough for your liking, refrigerate. Enjoy your own homemade probiotic delicacy!

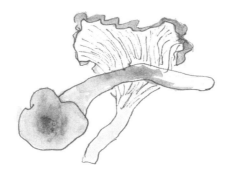

Matsutake Kim Chee

Be cautious in using mushrooms in kim chee. Being high in protein, they might become toxic if the wrong bacteria got into the batch. Be sure the mushrooms are young and in good condition. If the kim chee smells or looks rotten, gets moldy or gets pink or yellow discoloration, discard it.

Makes 1 quart

5 to 6 cups Napa cabbage, sliced crosswise

1 cup thinly sliced, young, fresh matsutake

1 onion, thinly sliced

1 clove garlic, minced

1 teaspoon minced fresh ginger

2 teaspoons red miso

1 to 2 teaspoons red pepper flakes or a few dried red peppers (or to taste)

1 tablespoon salt

Mix all ingredients in a large bowl. Let stand ½ hour. Pack into a wide mouth quart mason jar or small kraut crock. Be sure cabbage is below liquid level. Screw lid on jar, loosely, or place follower and weight in crock. Allow to ferment at room temperature. Taste daily, using a clean spoon or fork to prevent contamination, until it is sour enough for your liking. Depending upon the ambient temperature this may take from 3 to 10 days. Refrigerate when ready. It will keep in the refrigerator for several weeks.

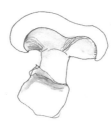

Sauces, Marinades and Gravies

Agaricus Agustus Alfredo Sauce

This recipe may be used with any species of Agaricus, *but the prince gives it a special flavor.*

Makes about 3 cups of sauce

1 tablespoon butter

2 cups fresh *Agaricus augustus*, chopped

¼ onion or 1 shallot, minced

¼ red bell pepper, chopped

2 cloves garlic, minced or pressed

2 cups milk or half and half

¼ cup grated provolone cheese

¼ cup grated Parmesan cheese

1 tablespoon cornstarch

1 tablespoon fresh minced basil

In a saucepan, sauté the mushrooms and onions in butter until the onions are transparent. Add bell pepper, stir once or twice, and then add garlic and sauté until fragrant. Add milk and cheeses, and heat until almost boiling. Mix cornstarch with 2 tablespoons of water and add, stirring constantly. Boil, stirring, for one minute; remove from heat, and stir in the basil. Serve over pasta.

Salmon Alfredo with Chanterelles or Hedgehogs

This recipe may be prepared using fresh salmon instead of canned. The flavor will be milder.

Makes about 3 cups sauce

1½ to 2 cups chopped chanterelles or hedgehogs

½ onion, chopped

1 tablespoon olive oil

2 cloves garlic, minced

1 (6 ounce) can of salmon with liquid

½ cup fresh or frozen green peas

¼ cup grated Parmesan cheese

½ cup plus 2 tablespoons milk

2 teaspoons cornstarch

1 tablespoon minced fresh basil or 1 teaspoon dried

½ teaspoon salt

In a saucepan, sauté the mushrooms with the onion in the olive oil until the mushrooms are well cooked and any water that has come out of them has evaporated. If using dried basil, add at this time. Add the garlic and sauté another minute.

Add the salmon with its juices, the Parmesan cheese, and peas to the pan and simmer a minute or two until peas are bright green. Add the ½ cup milk. While the pot returns to a simmer, stir together, in a small cup, the cornstarch and the 2 tablespoons milk. Stir this blend rapidly into the sauce, stirring constantly to make a smooth sauce. Simmer, stirring, until thickened, then continue for 1 minute more, and remove from heat. Add the salt and the fresh basil.

Serve immediately over cooked pasta.

Super-Easy Vegetarian Mushroom Pasta Sauce

Serves 4 to 6

2 to 3 cups wild mushrooms

1 tablespoon olive oil

1 (15 to 24-ounce) bottle commercial pasta sauce

Sauté the mushrooms in a saucepan in oil until they are done. Add the pasta sauce, heat to a simmer, and serve over pasta, garnished with Parmesan cheese.

Easy Porcini Spaghetti Sauce with Meatballs

Serves 4 to 6

2 to 3 cups diced fresh *Boletus edulis* or ½ cup dried, cut into pieces with scissors

1 onion, chopped

2 tablespoons olive oil

1 pound ground meat (hamburger, sausage or a blend)

1 (15 to 24-ounce) bottle red spaghetti sauce

¼ cup white wine

1 bay leaf

Sauté the onions and fresh mushrooms (do not add dried at this time) in olive oil in a saucepan over medium heat until the onions are translucent. Meanwhile, roll the meat into balls, and add them about halfway through the cooking. Add the spaghetti sauce, dried mushrooms, wine, and bay leaf, simmer for 15 minutes, and serve over pasta, with Parmesan cheese.

Red Spaghetti Sauce with Boletes

Serves 3 to 4

⅔ cup diced eggplant (optional) plus 1 teaspoon salt

2 cups diced fresh boletes (or ½ cup dried, torn into pieces)

½ carrot, chopped

½ onion chopped

½ teaspoon basil

¼ teaspoon thyme

⅛ teaspoon oregano

2 tablespoon olive oil

½ cup ground beef (optional)

½ red bell pepper, chopped

1 (6-ounce) can tomato paste

2 cups chopped fresh tomatoes or 1 (14-ounce) can

1 bay leaf

¼ cup white wine

If using eggplant, put it in a small bowl and sprinkle it with salt. Toss and let stand for 20 minutes. Rinse the eggplant.

In a large saucepan, sauté the fresh mushrooms, carrot, onion, eggplant and herbs, in olive oil over medium heat until onions are translucent. Add the ground beef and break it up with a spatula into small pieces. Stir until meat is cooked through. Add the peppers and sauté for one minute more.

Add the tomatoes (and their juice if canned), the wine, dried mushrooms (if using), and the bay leaf. Simmer for 15 minutes. Stir in tomato paste, and serve over pasta with Parmesan cheese.

Coral Mushroom/Squid Pasta Sauce

Begin this recipe the night before.

Serves 2
1 cup white wine
1 tablespoon lemon juice
½ teaspoon salt
2 sprigs fresh rosemary
2 cloves garlic
1 large young *Ramaria botrytis* (about 1½ cups, cut into chunks)
1 tablespoon olive oil
¼ onion, chopped
1 stalk celery, chopped
1 (8-ounce) can tomato sauce
6 squid
¼ cup grated mozzarella or jack cheese
¼ cup sour cream

Combine wine, lemon juice, salt, and rosemary. Slice garlic and add. Marinate the coral mushrooms in this mixture overnight.

In a saucepan, sauté the marinated mushrooms and the onion in olive oil for about 5 minutes. Remove the rosemary from the marinade and pour the marinade into the saucepan. Add the celery. Simmer until the liquid is nearly evaporated. Meanwhile clean the squid and cut the mantles into rings. When the pan is nearly dry, throw in the squid tentacles and mantles and stir-fry for a few minutes. Add the tomato sauce and simmer until sauce has thickened to a good consistency. Add the grated cheese and sour cream. Remove from heat, and serve over pasta, with Parmesan cheese. If black squid ink pasta is available, it can be fun to use.

Chanterelle Pesto

Makes 2½ to 3 cups

½ cup nuts (cashews, walnuts, almonds, hazelnuts, or pine nuts)

¼ red onion

2 cloves garlic

½ cup grated Parmesan cheese

1 cup fresh basil leaves (packed)

1½ cups chanterelles

¼ cup olive oil

¼ teaspoon salt

In a food processor chop the nuts, onion, and garlic until it attains the consistency of coarse meal. (If using pine nuts, process only the onion and garlic and add the nuts whole.) Put nut mixture into a bowl and add the grated parmesan cheese. Process the basil leaves until they are finely chopped and add them to the bowl with the nut, garlic and onion mixture. Then stir in the salt and olive oil.

Rough chop the chanterelles and dry-sauté them until their moisture exudes and evaporates. When mushrooms are done, run them through the food processor until they are smooth and then stir them into the pesto mixture. Serve immediately over hot pasta.

Mushroom Enchilada Sauce

Save the liquids drained from this recipe, in case you need to thin the sauce at the end.

Makes 2½ to 3 cups

1 dried ancho chile

¼ cup dried porcini, or 2 tablespoons dried, smoked mushrooms (see recipe on page 255)

1 cup boiling water

1 (15-ounce) can fire roasted tomatoes or about 1 pound fresh tomatoes

2 jalapeño peppers or 2 dried chipotle chiles

½ onion

½ teaspoon salt

2 cloves garlic

2 tablespoons butter

4 teaspoons flour or 2 teaspoons cornstarch

Preheat the broiler if you are using any fresh tomatoes or jalapeños. Toast any dried chiles in a dry frying pan, pressing down on them with a spatula for a few seconds. Then remove and discard the seeds. Put them in a bowl with the dried mushrooms, and pour hot water over them. Let them sit for 15 minutes.

Roast any fresh tomatoes and fresh chilies under the broiler, turning them until their skins bubble evenly. Remove them from the broiler, cool them enough to handle them, and peel them.

Put the drained rehydrated chiles and mushrooms, the broiled and peeled jalapeños and tomatoes, the drained canned tomatoes, the onions, salt and garlic into a food processor or blender, reserving drained liquids. Purée. If you are using a blender, add some of the reserved liquids as needed to thin it enough to purée well.

If you are using flour as a thickener, melt the butter in a saucepan and stir in the flour. Cook over medium-low heat until it's bubbly, then add the purée a bit at a time while stirring, allowing it to return to a boil between additions.

If you are using cornstarch, mix the cornstarch into 2 tablespoons of reserved liquid. Put puree and butter into saucepan, bring to a simmer, and stir in the cornstarch mixture. Simmer until sauce thickens slightly.

Candy Cap Barbeque Sauce

Makes 1¾ cups, enough for one chicken

1 cup ketchup

½ cup fruit juice (pineapple, orange, or whatever you have on hand)

3 tablespoons rice vinegar

2 tablespoons brown sugar

1 tablespoon ground candy cap mushrooms

Mix all ingredients well. May be use as a marinade or a condiment. May be canned for later use, or kept in the refrigerator for up to 3 weeks.

To marinate meat, coat chicken, pork or beef pieces. Allow to marinate at least 4 hours or overnight. Grill, or bake in the sauce and enjoy!

Matsutake Teriyaki Marinade

This marinade is less sweet than the candy cap one. If matsutakes are not in season, you can make a more subtle version with just the matsutake sake and without the additional fresh mushroom.

Makes about 2½ cups

1 cup tamari or shoyu

1 cup matsutake sake (see recipe on page 212)

½ cup chopped matsutake

1 clove garlic

2 thin slices ginger

¼ cup sugar

Put all ingredients in a blender and puree. Marinate meats, tofu or pig's ear mushrooms, in the refrigerator, for a minimum of 4 hours and up to 3 days for best penetration of flavor.

Candy Cap Teriyaki Marinade

Makes 1 cup

⅓ cup candy cap syrup (see recipe on page 219)

⅓ cup Japanese soy sauce (shoyu or tamari)

⅓ cup mirin or sherry

2 cloves garlic

1 teaspoon minced ginger

Combine syrup, soy sauce and wine. Mince, press or crush the garlic and add, along with the ginger. Marinate fish and chopped or thinly sliced meats for 1 to 6 hours, larger cuts of meat 3 to 5 days, in the refrigerator. Meat may be cooked in the marinade to strengthen the flavors and make a sauce.

Candy Cap Teriyaki Sauce

Makes 1 cup

1 recipe Candy Cap Teriyaki Marinade (above)

1 teaspoon cornstarch

2 tablespoon water

Bring the marinade to a simmer in a small saucepan over medium heat. In a small bowl or cup, stir the cornstarch and water together, then stir them into the marinade, stirring constantly until the marinade thickens into a sauce.

Matsutake Teriyaki Sauce

Substitute Matsutake Teriyaki Marinade (previous page) for the Candy Cap Marinade in the recipe above.

Triple Chanterelle Sauce

This is a recipe for mild winter years or areas where there is an overlap in the golden and black chanterelle crops. Otherwise, you can use dried blacks, using ½ the volume and soak them in hot water, first, for 15 minutes. The excess soaking water may be used as the "water or stock" component of the recipe.

Makes 3 to 4 cups
1 cup golden chanterelles
1 cup white chanterelles
1 cup black chanterelles
2 teaspoons olive oil
2 cloves garlic, minced
¼ cup dry white wine
water or stock
1 tablespoon cornstarch
1 teaspoon miso
juice of ½ lemon
salt to taste

Finely chop the three types of chanterelles and sauté them in a saucepan over medium heat in the olive oil with the garlic, until they exude their water. Add the wine. If the chanterelles were waterlogged from rain, they may need no additional water or stock. If they are drier, add enough water or stock to cover the chanterelles, and make about 3 cups. Bring the pot to a boil. Stir the cornstarch into ¼ cup cold water or stock, and pour it into the mushroom mixture, stirring constantly until it thickens. Remove from heat. Stir the miso into the lemon juice, then stir it into the sauce, along with salt to taste. Serve with fish, chicken, or vegetables, or use as a low-fat, mushroomy alternative to hollandaise sauce.

Porcini Gravy

Makes about 3 cups gravy

½ cup dried porcini, torn into small pieces

1 cup chicken or turkey broth

¼ cup chopped onion

4 tablespoons butter (or chicken or turkey fat)

Giblets from chicken or turkey, minced

1 clove garlic, minced

1 teaspoon thyme

¼ teaspoon sage or oregano or rosemary

¼ cup flour

About 2 cups milk

1 teaspoon salt or to taste

Put the mushrooms and broth in a small saucepan, bring to a simmer, cover and turn off heat.

In a frying pan, sauté the onions and giblets in butter or fat. Add the herbs and garlic and sauté for a minute or two, until the garlic is fragrant. Sprinkle the flour in lightly, stirring until flour begins to brown. Stir in half the broth and mushrooms, as the gravy thickens, stir in the other half. Then stir in milk slowly, a little at a time, allowing the gravy to thicken between each addition. When gravy is the appropriate thickness, allow it to come to a simmer for a few minutes, and add more milk if necessary. Salt to taste.

Chanterelle Gravy

This is a good, basic gravy to serve with turkey or chicken. It can be made with many other species of mushroom. It can also be made to accompany roast pork or beef. Just substitute the drippings of whatever meat you are using, skimming the fat to cook the mushrooms, and using the juices to replace the turkey drippings. Substitute rosemary for the sage, and omit the giblets.

Makes 3 to 4 cups

2 cups minced chanterelles

¼ cup minced onion

¼ cup plus 2 tablespoons chicken or turkey fat

Giblets from chicken or turkey, minced (optional)

2 cloves garlic, minced

½ teaspoon thyme

¼ teaspoon sage

¼ cup flour

½ cup chicken or turkey drippings, skimmed of fat or 1 cup broth, skimmed

2 to 3 cups milk

salt and pepper to taste

Sauté the chanterelles and onions in the 2 tablespoons of fat until they are cooked and the water has evaporated out of the mushrooms. Add the giblets, garlic and herbs; sauté 2 minutes. Add the remaining ¼ cup fat and stir in the flour. Stir constantly, until the flour begins to brown. Slowly add the broth or meat juices, stirring constantly. Continue by adding milk, a little at a time, allowing the gravy to begin to thicken between each addition. Add milk until the gravy is the desired consistency at a simmer. Season to taste with salt and pepper.

Vegetarian Gravy with Sweetbread Mushrooms

This gravy may be made vegan by using only vegetable broth and leaving out the milk. It may be made gluten-free by substituting a gluten-free flour for the wheat flour, but the thickening ability may be less, so it may make a smaller volume. Another gluten-free option is thickening it with cornstarch, using 1 tablespoonful, and mixing it with ¼ cup cold milk or broth. After sautéing the mushrooms, onions, garlic and herbs, add 1½ cups broth or milk and broth combination. Bring to a simmer and add the cornstarch mixture, stirring constantly until it thickens, then add more milk or broth as needed for proper consistency.

Makes 1½ to 2 cups

1 cup sweetbread mushrooms, finely chopped

2 tablespoons minced onion

2 tablespoons butter or oil

1 clove garlic, minced

¼ teaspoon thyme

⅛ teaspoon sage

2 tablespoons flour

½ to 2 cups vegetable broth

½ to 1 cup milk (optional)

salt and pepper to taste

Sauté mushrooms and onions in butter or oil. When onions become translucent, add garlic and herbs. After one minute, add flour and sauté, stirring, until flour begins to brown. Slowly stir in ½ cup broth. As it thickens, stir in more broth or milk until desired consistency is reached at a simmer. Season to taste with salt and pepper.

Man on Horseback Gravy

Makes about 2 cups

6 *Tricholoma flavovirens*, finely chopped (about a cup)

2 tablespoons chicken fat, oil or butter

Pinch of thyme

1 tablespoon flour

½ cup chicken broth

1 cup milk

¼ to ½ teaspoon salt, or to taste

Sauté the mushrooms in the fat until just done. Add the thyme and flour. Cook, stirring until the flour begins to brown. Add the broth a little at a time, stirring it into the flour mixture. Then add milk a little at a time, stirring constantly, and allowing the mixture to come back to a boil between additions, until the gravy is of the desired consistency. Add salt to taste.

Breads

Mushroom Garlic Bread

Makes one loaf

One loaf unsliced sourdough or sweet French bread

One recipe of either version of Mushroom Butter (see recipe on page 39)

Preheat the oven to 400° F. Slice loaf in half horizontally. Spread butter on both halves. Cut the half loaves into slices, not cutting clear through the crust, so slices may be torn off when it's done. Place both halves crust side down on a cookie sheet. Cover with foil. Bake for 20 minutes. Slice and serve.

Candy Cap Scones

Makes 8 to 10

1 tablespoon ground, dried candy caps

1½ cups unbleached flour

¼ cup sugar

½ teaspoon salt

½ teaspoon baking soda

¼ cup butter (not softened)

½ cup yogurt

Preheat the oven to 425° F. Grease a cookie sheet.

Combine the dry ingredients in a mixing bowl. Cut the butter into the flour mixture with a pastry knife or a strong fork until the flakes are about the size of peas. Fold the yogurt in until it is just incorporated—do not over-mix. Using a tablespoon or small serving spoon, immediately spoon out heaping spoonfuls of dough onto the cookie sheet, about 1½ inch apart. Bake scones at 425° F for 15 to 20 minutes or until golden brown.

Candy Cap Cornbread

This is a sweet cornbread, which is good both with or without the bacon.

Makes 16 2-inch-square servings

¾ cup cornmeal

¾ cup unbleached or whole wheat flour

¼ cup ground dried candy caps

¼ cup sugar

½ teaspoon salt

1 teaspoon baking soda

2 tablespoons melted butter or bacon grease

1 egg

½ cup milk

¼ cup yogurt

¼ cup cooked, crumbled bacon (optional)

Grease an 8-inch-square baking pan and preheat the oven to 425° F.

Combine the dry ingredients in a mixing bowl. Blend in the melted butter or fat with a fork.

In a small bowl, beat the egg with a fork or whisk, and beat in the milk. Fold the egg mixture into the dry ingredients. Fold in the yogurt and bacon. Do not over-mix. Pour the batter immediately into the prepared pan, and bake it at 425° F for 25 to 30 minutes, or until the top is golden and set, and the edges begin to shrink from the sides of the pan. Cool for 5 to 10 minutes, then remove from the pan. Serve warm or cold.

Corny Candy Cap Corn Bread

Follow the above recipe, but substitute one 14 to 15 ounce can of corn kernels (not creamed), including the juice, for the milk.

Pizza Dough

Makes a crust for one 12 to 14-inch pizza

⅔ cup warm water

1 teaspoon dry active yeast

1 teaspoon sugar

½ teaspoon salt

¼ cup powdered, dried Boletus or other mushroom powder (optional)

2 to 2½ cups flour

olive oil

Put the warm water in a large bowl with the sugar and the yeast. Let it sit in a warm place for 15 minutes or until it looks bubbly. Add the salt and powdered dried mushroom, and stir in just enough flour that the dough can be kneaded. Turn it out onto a floured board, and knead in flour until the dough is elastic and no longer sticky, but still soft. Oil the bowl, and replace the dough in the bowl, oiling the top of the dough, also. Allow it to rise in a warm place until doubled in size, 1 to 1½ hours. Punch down and knead again. Then throw out, roll or stretch into a pizza crust shape.

Mushroom Bread

This is a French style bread. You may use either white or whole wheat flour, or a blend of the two. You may add a sourdough starter, incorporating it in the sponge stage. This can be baked in two loaf pans, or formed into one or two free-form loaves and baked on a cookie sheet.

Makes 2 loaves.

2 cups dried boletes, black trumpets, or other dried mushrooms

3 cups boiling water

1 onion

4 cloves garlic

2 tablespoons olive oil

1 package dry active yeast

2 tablespoons sugar

½ cup pitted Kalamata olives (optional)

4 to 5 cups flour

2 teaspoons salt

Cut the dried mushrooms into bits with scissors. Put them in a bowl and pour the boiling water over them. Cover and let stand until the water is lukewarm.

Meanwhile, peel and finely chop the onion. Sauté it in one tablespoon of the olive oil until pieces become translucent, then begin to caramelize. Mince the garlic and add, sautéing a few minutes more. Remove from heat and transfer to a small bowl.

When the mushrooms have cooled to lukewarm, drain off and reserve the liquid. Measure out 2½ cups of liquid. If there is not enough, add more warm water. Stir in the sugar and yeast, and let sit in a warm place about 10 minutes or until it begins to froth.

Combine the drained mushrooms with the onions. Chop the olives, if using, and add them to the mushroom mixture. Set aside.

Mix one cup of flour with the yeast mixture in a large bowl. Put in a warm place and allow to rise ½ hour. Stir in 2 more cups of flour. Add more flour, a little at a time, until it is less sticky and can be kneaded. Turn the dough out onto a heavily floured board and knead in flour until it looses most of its stickiness.

Continue to knead, adding a little more flour when necessary, until the dough is smooth and elastic.

Oil the bowl, return the dough to the bowl, and allow to rise in a warm place for 1 to 2 hours, or until it has doubled in bulk. Punch down and knead out air. Return the dough to the bowl and let it rise again until doubled. Punch down and knead again.

Grease the pans.

Roll the dough out on a lightly floured board, to the shape of a rectangle, 16 to 18 inches long. Spread the mushroom mixture over the surface and roll up, starting from one of the long sides, to make a roll 16 to 18 inches long. If you are going to make two loaves, cut the roll in half, and press each piece into the bottom of a greased loaf pan, or round the ends and place them on two greased cookie sheets, making sure they have room to expand. If you choose to make one large loaf, round the ends and put it on a large greased cookie sheet, placing it on the diagonal.

Allow the loaves to rise in a warm place for ½ hour to 45 minutes, until doubled in size. Mid-way through the rising, set the oven to 350° F to preheat. Bake the loaves for about an hour, or until the tops are golden and the loaf sounds hollow when tapped. Allow them to cool in the pans for 5 minutes, then remove the loaves from the pans and cool on a rack or wooden board.

Easy Chanterelle Drop Biscuits

Makes 1 dozen

1 teaspoon olive oil

1 cup minced chanterelles

1 tablespoon sausage or finely chopped bacon (optional)

1½ cups flour

1 teaspoon salt

1½ teaspoons baking powder or ¾ teaspoon baking soda

3 tablespoons butter (cold)

1 teaspoon thyme or basil

¼ cup grated cheddar cheese

¾ cup buttermilk or sour milk

Sauté the chanterelles and meat in the olive oil until any water they exude has evaporated. Allow to cool completely. Preheat oven to 425 F. Combine the flour, salt and baking powder or soda. Cut in the butter with a pastry cutter or a fork. Toss in the chanterelles, herbs and cheese. Mix in the milk. Put out by large spoonfuls onto a greased baking sheet and bake 10 to 15 minutes, until golden brown on top. Serve warm or cold.

Soups

Cream of Mushroom Soup

This recipe is especially good with the almond flavored Agaricus augustus, A. arvensis, *etc., but is also excellent with other* Agaricus *species, chanterelles, black trumpets, and may be used with any mushroom for subtle flavor variations.*

Serves 4

2 cups chopped fresh mushrooms

½ onion, chopped

2 tablespoons butter

2 cloves garlic, minced or pressed

½ teaspoon thyme

1 quart milk

½ to 1 teaspoon salt, to taste

2 tablespoons cornstarch

Sauté the mushroom and onion in the butter in a frying pan until the onion is slightly caramelized. Add the garlic and thyme. Sauté a minute or two more.

Combine half the mushroom mixture with 2 cups of milk in the blender and purée until smooth. Pour the purée into a large saucepan. Add the remaining mushroom mixture, remaining milk, and salt to the saucepan, without puréeing. Heat until nearly boiling, stirring frequently. Mix the cornstarch with ¼ cup water and add to soup, stirring constantly as the soup begins to thicken. Bring to a boil for one minute, stirring constantly, and serve.

Extra Rich Cream of Mushroom Soup

For this delicious version, use the recipe on the previous page, but boil a medium potato and add it to the blender with 2 tablespoons of Parmesan cheese and half the mushroom mixture. Then substitute 1½ cups half and half plus ½ cup sour cream for 2 cups of the milk in the recipe above. Follow instructions for previous soup, but omit the corn starch.

Cream of Augustus Soup

Recipe by Christine Schomer.

Serves 4 to 6

1 large *Agaricus augustus*, chopped

½ cup butter

¼ cup plus 2 tablespoons flour

¼ cup minced onion

2 cloves garlic, minced

3 cups milk

3 cups water

¼ cup sherry, or to taste

Salt and pepper to taste

In a skillet, melt 2 tablespoons of the butter, over moderate heat. Sauté the mushrooms, onion and garlic until the onions are translucent, and the mushrooms are limp. Remove from heat.

In a soup pot, melt the remaining butter over moderate heat. Sift the flour into the butter. Use a whisk to blend thoroughly, and continue stirring until the mixture looks golden, but not quite brown. Have the milk and water in a pitcher by the stove. Add the liquid slowly, while stirring with a whisk, beating out any lumps that form before adding all the liquid.

Then add the mushroom mixture, the sherry and the salt and pepper. Reduce the heat and continue to warm the soup slowly, stirring often, for about 15 minutes. Do not let the soup boil as it will separate. Serve with bread sticks.

Boletus Barley Soup

Recipe by Irina Valioulina. This is a Russian-style soup.

Serves 4

¾ cup barley

1 cup dried *Boletus edulis*

½ onion

1 teaspoon butter or oil

2 large potatoes

1 teaspoon salt or to taste

½ cup sour cream for garnish

In a saucepan, boil the barley in a quart of water for 30 minutes. Drain.

While the barley is cooking, make a mushroom stock by putting the boletus into another pan with 2 cups of water. Bring it to a boil, cover and simmer for 10 minutes. Strain the stock through a cheese cloth into a soup pot, squeezing out as much liquid as possible.

Sauté the onions in a small frying pan in the butter until they begin to brown. Add them to the soup pot, then put a cup of water into the frying pan, and stir it with a spatula over medium heat until any bits of onion and flavor have transferred into the water. Add this water to the soup pot.

Dice the potatoes and add them to the soup pot. Chop the boiled boletus from the cheesecloth and add it back in, and add the drained barley and the salt. Add enough water to cover all the ingredients. Bring to a boil, turn down, cover and simmer for 20 minutes. Serve garnished with a spoonful of sour cream.

Boletus Borscht

Yellow feet, chanterelles, or any other savory mushroom may be substituted for the boletes; use 2 to 3 cups fresh mushrooms, and sauté them with the onions.

Serves 8

I onion, chopped

3 carrots, grated

2 tablespoons butter or oil

2 stalks celery

4 cloves garlic

1 quart vegetable or beef stock

2 to 3 tablespoons red wine vinegar

2 large beets

3 potatoes

½ cup dried *Boletus edulis*

½ head cabbage

1 teaspoon salt or to taste

2 tablespoons dill weed

1 teaspoon caraway seed

½ cup sour cream for garnish

Sauté the onion and carrots in the butter until the onions are translucent. Slice the celery and add; sauté 3 minutes. Mince the garlic and add and sauté one more minute. Set aside.

Put the stock into a large pot with a quart of water, bring to a boil. Cut the beets into julienne, and add them to the pot. Dice the potatoes and add. Cut the dried mushrooms into pieces and add them. Slice the cabbage and add it. Simmer 15 minutes, then add the sautéed ingredients and simmer a few more minutes to meld flavors.

Yogurt Mushroom Soup

This recipe is reprinted from Gathered Mushroom Recipes, *a collection of recipes by Teresa Sholars' 1981 mushroom class at the Mendocino Coast Branch of College of the Redwoods. You may use most mushroom species in this recipe, including Fistulina hepatica.*

Serves 6

¼ cup butter

1 onion, chopped

6 green onions, sliced

¾ pound of mushrooms (about 3 cups, sliced, depending on water content)

2 teaspoons paprika

¼ cup flour

6 cups chicken broth

2 egg yolks

1½ cups yogurt

¼ teaspoon dill weed

salt to taste

In a soup pot, melt the butter and sauté the onions, green onions and mushrooms until they are well cooked. Stir in the paprika and the flour, and cook, stirring, for a few minutes.

Stir in the chicken broth, a little at a time. Heat until it comes to a boil. Beat the egg yolks, and stir them into the soup. Bring back to a simmer. Turn off heat, and stir in the yogurt and dill. Salt to taste, and serve.

Black Trumpet Cream of Nettle or Spinach Soup

Winter foragers' delight: nettles and blacks.

Serves 2 to 3

2 cups fresh (or 1 cup dried) black chanterelles

2 cups young nettle tips or spinach leaves or a combination

1 cup water or broth

2 cups milk (or half and half)

1½ teaspoons salt, or to taste

2 tablespoons cornstarch

Sour cream for garnish

Put the nettles (handle with gloves) or spinach in a blender with the water or broth. Blend until coarsely puréed. Pour into a 2 quart soup pot.

Put the chanterelles into the blender with the milk. Blend on low speed until minced. Pour into the soup pot. Add the salt. Heat to boiling. Blend the cornstarch into ¼ cup cold water and add to the soup, stirring constantly until it returns to the boil. Stir while boiling for 1 minute, and serve, garnishing each bowl with a dollop of sour cream.

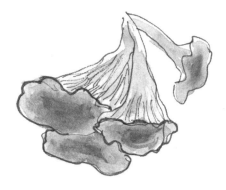

French Onion Soup with The Prince or Matsutake

Serves 4

2 onions, sliced

2 tablespoons butter

1 cup chopped *Agaricus augustus* or matsutake

4 cups water or unsalted stock

1 teaspoon salt or to taste

4 toasted slices baguette or 1 cup French bread croutons

¼ cup Parmesan, Asiago, or mozzarella cheese

Slice the onions. Place the butter in a 6-cup soup pot and sauté the onions, stirring frequently until they are golden. Add the mushrooms and continue to cook until the onions are caramelized and brown. Add water or stock and the salt, and bring to a boil. Boil 10 minutes. Divide the bread between bowls, fill with soup, and top with grated cheese.

French Onion Soup with Porcini or Candy Caps

This soup is excellent with porcini, and amazing with candy caps.

Serves 4

2 onions, sliced

2 tablespoons butter

2 to 4 tablespoons chopped dried porcini or minced dried candy caps

4 cups water or stock

1 teaspoon salt or to taste

4 toasted slices baguette or 1 cup French bread croutons

¼ cup grated Parmesan, Asiago, or mozzarella cheese

Slice the onions. Place the butter in a 6-cup soup pot and sauté the onions, stirring frequently until they are good and brown. Add water or stock, the mushrooms, and salt, and bring to a boil. Boil 10 minutes. Divide bread between bowls, fill with soup, and top with 1 tablespoon grated cheese.

Chanterelle Soup

This recipe is reprinted from Gathered Mushroom Recipes, *a collection of recipes by Teresa Sholars' 1981 mushroom class at the Mendocino Coast Branch of College of the Redwoods.*

Serves 4

1 quart chicken broth

1 onion, chopped

1 cup celery, chopped

1 pound of chanterelles (about 4 cups, depending on water content)

¼ cup butter

¼ cup white wine

¼ teaspoon nutmeg

Pinch of ground cloves

Salt to taste

Boil the onion and celery in the chicken stock in a large sauce pan until tender. Meanwhile, chop the chanterelles and cook them gently in the butter, in a lidded frying pan, until the mushrooms have exuded their water and are cooked through.

Purée half the mushrooms and all of the stock in a blender. Return soup to sauce pan and add the remaining mushrooms and their juices, the wine, nutmeg and cloves. Salt to taste. Bring to a simmer, and serve.

Matsutake Soup

Serves 2

1 tablespoon coconut oil (or other light oil of your choice)

4 matsutake buttons, sliced

2 stalks celery, chopped

1 small burdock root, finely chopped (about ¼ cup)

1 carrot, thinly sliced

1 clove garlic, minced

1 small head bok choy (or 8 large leaves), sliced

¼ cup dried seaweed

2 cups vegetable stock (you may substitute chicken or other)

½ red bell pepper, sliced thinly

¼ lemon

Cilantro for garnish (optional)

In a saucepan, sauté the matsutakes in the oil for a few minutes until they begin to soften. Stir in the celery, then the carrot, the burdock root, and the garlic. Add the bok choy and sauté a minute more.

Add the stock and seaweed, and simmer, covered, for 5 minutes more, or until vegetables are done, but still al dente. Turn off the heat and add the slivered red bell pepper. Cover pan for a minute to let pepper soften while you prepare 2 soup bowls. Serve, adding a squeeze of lemon to each bowl. Optional: garnish with a few cilantro leaves.

Matsutake Chicken Soup with Egg Noodles

Serves 10 to 12

½ gallon chicken stock

1 recipe (follows) egg noodles, or 1 12-ounce package store-bought

3 cups chopped matsutake mushrooms

1 cup chopped celery

1 onion, chopped

6 cloves garlic, minced or pressed

3 cups chopped boned chicken

¼ cup miso

Salt to taste

Heat chicken stock to boiling, add raw noodles, then matsutakes.

If chicken is raw, add it now. If cooked, add when nearly done. Add celery, onion, and garlic. Cook until noodles and vegetables are done, about 15-20 minutes. If using commercial dried noodles add them at a time appropriate to the cooking time on the package. Mix ½ cup of the hot broth into the miso to soften it, then add to soup. Salt to taste.

Egg Noodles

1 egg

1 tablespoon water

1 teaspoon salt

1 to 1½ cups all purpose flour, plus flour for rolling out the dough (whole wheat makes grainy noodles)

Optional: for mushroom noodles, you may add 2 to 4 tablespoons powdered dried mushrooms in place of part of the flour.

Mix egg, water and salt. (If using powdered mushroom, add it now, subtracting that amount from the following flour.) Stir in ¾ cup flour, then mix in/ knead in more flour, a little at a time, until you have a non-sticky dough, firmer than bread dough, but not tough. The exact amount will vary as eggs vary in size. Roll out on a well-floured board.

When the dough is as thin as you can easily get it, flour the top surface well, fold in half, and roll out again, checking to be sure the halves do not stick together, and adding more flour as necessary. Then flour the top and starting at one end, fold over 3 to 4 inches of dough. Fold again. Repeat the process, folding over and over until you have a long rectangle of layered dough. Cut in half the long way, then slice crosswise to form ¼-inch slices for the noodles.

Separate the noodles before putting them into the broth. Cook about 20 minutes

Matsutake Won Ton Soup

Serves 6 to 8

2 tablespoons chicken fat or peanut or coconut oil

2 cups sliced matsutakes

3 cloves garlic, minced

1 tablespoon chopped ginger

3 green onions, chopped

2 quarts chicken broth

1 recipe matsutake won tons (see recipe on page 44)

1 cup chopped bok choy or chinese cabbage

½ of an 8-ounce can bamboo shoots

Put the fat or oil in a large soup pot and heat over medium heat. Add the mushrooms and sauté until they soften. Add the garlic, ginger and onions. Sauté a few more minutes. Add the chicken broth, and bring to a boil. Simmer 15 minutes. Add the won tons, return to a simmer. Add the bok choy and bamboo shoots, simmer 5 minutes or until the bok choy and won tons are done.

Porcini Dumplings

These are egg dumplings to be boiled in soup. For filled dumplings, see Matsutake Won Tons recipe on page 44.

2 eggs
1 cup water
1 teaspoon vinegar
¼ cup ground dried porcini
1¼ cup flour
½ teaspoon salt
¼ teaspoon baking soda

Have the soup or broth at a simmer. Beat the eggs. Beat in the water and vinegar. Blend in the porcini powder and 1 cup of the flour. Combine the remaining flour with the salt and soda and stir it quickly in to the batter. Drop the batter by spoonfuls into the soup. Simmer them about 15 minutes.

Mushroom Matzo Balls

There are three variations here: using dried ground mushrooms, which does not significantly affect the texture of the balls, and using chopped dried or fresh mushrooms, which, depending on the mushroom species, will affect the texture. You may use porcini, agaricus, chanterelles, hedgehogs or matsutake, and other species also.

Makes 6 to 8 balls

Matzo Balls with Dried Ground Mushrooms

2 tablespoons ground dried mushrooms

¼ cup plus 1 tablespoon hot chicken stock or hot water

2 large eggs

2 tablespoons melted chicken fat, butter or vegetable oil

½ cup matzo meal

1 teaspoon salt (optional)

Combine the mushrooms and the hot stock or water to allow the mushrooms to reconstitute for a few minutes.

Meanwhile, beat the eggs and fat or oil together with a fork. Stir in the matzo meal and salt, then mix in the dried mushrooms with their soaking liquid, and the 3 tablespoons stock or water. Chill for ½ hour.

Bring 1½ to 2 quarts of water or stock to a boil in a large pot. With wet hands, roll teaspoons of the dough into balls about 1 inch in diameter. (They will double in size as they cook.) Drop them one at a time into the boiling water. Reduce heat to a simmer; cover and simmer 30 to 40 minutes. If you roll the balls larger than one inch diameter, they will need to cook longer. You may check for doneness by cutting a ball in half. If the center is darker than the outer portion, they are not yet done. If you cook the balls in the soup stock, you may add the vegetables and meat after the matzo balls have cooked a half hour. If you cook the balls in water, remove them from the water with a slotted spoon and serve them in chicken, vegetable or mushroom soup.

Matzo Balls with Minced Dried Mushrooms

2 tablespoons minced dried mushrooms

¼ cup plus 1 tablespoon hot chicken stock or hot water

2 large eggs

2 tablespoons melted chicken fat, butter or vegetable oil

½ cup matzo meal

1 teaspoon salt (optional)

Combine the mushrooms and the hot stock or water to allow the mushrooms to reconstitute for a few minutes.

Meanwhile, beat the eggs and fat or oil together with a fork. Stir in the matzo meal and salt, then mix in the dried mushrooms with their soaking liquid. Chill for ½ hour.

Follow the directions above for cooking and serving.

Matzo Balls with Fresh Mushrooms

¼ cup minced fresh (or frozen) mushrooms

3 tablespoons cold chicken stock or water

2 large eggs

2 tablespoons melted chicken fat, butter or vegetable oil

½ cup matzo meal

1 teaspoon salt (optional)

Beat the eggs and the fat or oil together with a fork. Stir in the matzo meal and salt, then mix in the fresh mushrooms and the 3 tablespoons stock or water. Chill for 15 minutes.

Follow the directions above for cooking and serving.

Chanterelle or Matsutake Chowder

Other mushrooms that go well in this recipe are shrimp russula, variegated russula, flat-topped club coral, cocorra, grisettes, lobster mushrooms and shaggy manes.

Serves 6 to 8

2 cups chanterelles or matsutakes, chopped

2 tablespoons butter

1 cup chopped onion

1 cup chopped celery

1 cup diced potatoes

1 bay leaf

1 12-ounce (or two 5-ounce) cans salmon or clams

2 teaspoons salt

2 tablespoons cornstarch

2 cups milk (may use half and half, or cream for richer soup)

Sauté the mushrooms, onion, celery, in butter until the onions are translucent. Add 2 cups of water, the bay leaf, and the potatoes. Simmer until the potatoes are nearly done.

Reduce to low heat. Add the canned salmon or clams, with their juice, the milk, and salt. Mix the cornstarch with ¼ cup cold water and when the soup comes to a simmer, stir it in rapidly until the soup returns to a simmer, and then serve.

Shaggy Leeks Soup

Serves 2

1 small leek, sliced

1 tablespoon butter

1 tablespoon coconut oil

6 shaggy mane mushrooms, sliced lengthwise

2 cups stock

1 teaspoon salt, or to taste

¼ cup sweet red pepper, chopped (optional)

½ cup cream or half-and-half (optional)

1 tablespoon cornstarch (optional)

Sauté the leeks in a saucepan, in the butter and coconut oil, over medium heat for 3 minutes. Lay the shaggy manes in a single layer over the leeks, and cover with a lid for 5 minutes. Add the stock and salt, cover, and bring to a boil. Add the red bell pepper and serve immediately for the clear soup version.

For a cream soup, stir in the cream, then mix the cornstarch in a few tablespoons cold water, and stir it into the soup when it comes back to a simmer. Simmer over low heat, stirring constantly, until it thickens, then 1 minute more.

Split Pea Soup With Pigs Ears

Start this recipe the night before serving, as the peas need to be soaked overnight.

Serves 4

1 cup split peas

2 cups stock

1 cup milk or cream

1 to 2 carrots, chopped

½ cup chopped smoked pig's ears (see recipe on page 255)

2 slices bacon, cooked and roughly chopped

½ onion, chopped

1 teaspoon salt

Soak the peas overnight in enough water to cover them by 1 inch. Drain.

Cook the peas until they are tender in 2 cups fresh water plus 2 cups stock, about 3 hours on the stove, or 6 hours in a crock pot.

Put the milk and ½ of the pea soup into a blender and purée.

To the remaining soup in the pot, add the carrots, mushrooms, bacon, and onion, and boil until all vegetables are tender, 15 to 20 minutes. Mix in the contents of blender and salt to taste.

Candy Cap Pumpkin Soup

Makes about 3 cups of soup

1 cup broth or stock

½ cup milk

1½ cups cooked pumpkin

½ cup fresh candy caps (¼ cup chopped dried)

1 teaspoon brown sugar

Salt to taste

Pinch nutmeg

¼ inch slice fresh ginger (optional)

wedge of lemon with peel (⅛ lemon, chopped, preferably organic)

Put all the ingredients in a blender. Purée. Heat the soup in a saucepan until it just boils, stirring frequently. Simmer for 5 minutes. Serve, garnished with a sprinkle of nutmeg.

Turkey Tail Broth

May be frozen for use when needed.

Makes 1 gallon

1 cup turkey tail mushrooms (you may substitute up to half *Ganoderma* spp.)

bones from a chicken or 1 quart vegetable trimmings

2 bay leaves

1 teaspoon dried oregano or a 6 to 8 inch sprig of fresh oregano

2 teaspoons dried thyme or 1 tablespoon fresh thyme

1 head of garlic

2 tablespoons apple cider vinegar

Put all ingredients into a large pot or crock pot with one gallon of water. Bring to boil. Simmer 4 to 6 hours on the stove or overnight in a crock pot, replacing water that boils away. Cool, skim the excess fat and strain out solids. Salt to taste and use as soup base.

Princely Toscana Soup

Serves 4

1 nice *Agaricus augustus* mushroom

½ onion

2 tablespoons olive oil

½ pound spicy sausage, preferably Italian

3 cloves garlic

½ teaspoon fennel seed or ¼ cup chopped fresh fennel or chervil

2 large potatoes

1 cup chopped chard or spinach

½ cup shelled green fava beans (optional)

2 cups milk

1 tablespoon cornstarch

1 teaspoon Bragg's Aminos or soy sauce

1 teaspoon salt or to taste

¼ cup Parmesan cheese, grated

Chop the mushroom and onion and sauté in a skillet in the olive oil until onions are translucent. Add the sausage. If they are in casings, cook them halfway, then pull them out and slice them and return them to the pan. Chop and add the garlic. Turn off when the sausage is done.

Meanwhile, dice and boil the potatoes in 3 cups water. If using fennel seed, boil it with the potatoes. When the potatoes are done, put the milk into a blender and spoon about ½ of the potatoes into the blender.

Put the rest of the potatoes back on the heat, adding the fava beans. Add the cornstarch to the blender, and puree. When the fava beans are about done, add the sautéed mixture. Spoon some of the hot water from the potatoes into the skillet and rinse the grease and flavor into the soup. Add the chard or spinach, and if using fresh chervil or fennel, add it now. Bring the soup back to a boil, and add the pureed mixture. Stir until it thickens, then comes to a boil. Remove from heat. Add the Bragg's or soy, the salt and the cheese. Serve.

Mushroom Cioppino

This soup may be made in advance up to the point of adding the fish. Refrigerate for a few hours to overnight to allow flavors to meld and finish cooking when ready to serve.

Serves 8 to 10

1 *Boletus mirabilis*, or other bolete, sliced (fresh or dried)

2 cups oyster mushrooms, deer mushrooms, blewits, or shaggy manes, sliced

2 cups chanterelles, hedgehogs, blacks, or yellow foot, sliced

2 pounds shellfish in their shells, well cleaned, such as clams or mussels

1 pound fish, filleted, such as rock fish, ling cod, or halibut, cut into bite sized pieces

1 pound large or medium shrimp, peeled and deveined

½ pound scallop meat, calamari, or squid

1 onion, quartered and sliced

1 large shallot or small leek, sliced

½ head of garlic, peeled and sliced

3 cups fresh tomatoes (preferably Romas, sliced) or 1 (28-ounce) can

2 carrots, sliced

2 stalks celery, sliced

¼ cup dried or 1 cup fresh tender seaweed such as nori, sea palm, sea lettuce, chopped

¼ cup Italian parsley, chopped

1 teaspoon basil

1 teaspoon oregano

½ teaspoon red pepper flakes

½ teaspoon rosemary

1 bay leaf

4 cups fish stock or two 8 ounce bottles of clam juice

juice and grated rind of ½ lemon

1 cup white wine

¼ cup olive oil

Put 1 inch of water in a pot. Heat to boiling. Add the shellfish. Cover and bring back to a rolling boil, then turn off heat. Set aside.

In a large pot, sauté the onions, carrots, celery, herbs, pepper flakes and bay leaf in the olive oil over medium heat taking care not to let the oil smoke. Add the *Boletus* (if using fresh) and the chanterelles or hedgehogs. When the onions get translucent, add the other fresh mushrooms, garlic, and shallot or leek. Cover the pot and stir frequently, sautéing a few minutes more. Add the stock and 2 cups of water (if using clam juice add 4 cups of water) and bring to a boil. If using any dried mushrooms, add them now. Simmer 10 minutes. If using large calamari, cut it into bite sized pieces. If using squid, clean, debeak, and remove cartilage and ink sacs. Cut them into pieces. If using sea scallops, sauté them until half done before adding. Add wine, fish, shrimp, scallops, calamari, squid, seaweed and tomatoes and simmer until fish is just done. Add shellfish (in their shells) and decant shellfish cooking water into the soup, leaving any sand in the pan. Add the parsley and lemon. Reheat if it has cooled too much, salt as needed, and serve with garlic bread.

Cold Avocado Soup with Clavariadelphus

Serves 2

1 large ripe avocado

3 *Clavariadelphus truncatus*, chopped

1 tablespoon butter

1 cup vegetable stock or chicken broth

¾ cup half and half

¼ cup sour cream

½ teaspoon salt

Paprika and cilantro for garnish (optional)

Sauté the *Clavariadelphus* in butter. Put avocado, stock, half and half, sour cream and salt in the blender. Purée. Stir in mushrooms, pour into bowls, and garnish with a sprinkle of paprika and a sprig of cilantro.

Thai Coconut Milk Soup with Wild Mushrooms

In Thai, this soup is called Tom Kha Gai, and usually contains several different kinds of Asian mushrooms.

Serves 8 to 10

1 chicken, cut up, bone in

1 gallon water or turkey tail broth (recipe page 96)

3 limes

1-inch piece fresh galangal or 2 teaspoons powdered

3 stalks lemon grass

4 Kaffir lime leaves, if available

3 carrots

1 small onion

1½ cups sliced matsutake or shiitake (fresh) or ¾ cup dried shiitake

1 cup sliced deer mushrooms, volvariella, blewits, chanterelles, or hedgehogs

1½ cups sliced agaricus, sweetbread mushroom, man on horseback or ½ cup dried bolete

2 green onions

2 serrano chilis or Thai bird peppers

½ cup chopped cilantro

¼ cup fish sauce

2 (15-ounce) cans coconut milk

Put the chicken, the water or broth, and the juice of one lime in a large pot or crock pot. If using any dried mushrooms, tear them into bits and add them at this time. Add thinly sliced galangal or galangal powder. Cut the lemon grass into one inch pieces and add, with the Kaffir lime leaves. Bring to a boil and simmer for about two hours. After simmering, chicken may be boned and the meat returned to the soup.

Chop the onion and slice the carrots and add them, along with the mushrooms, to the soup. Simmer for 15 minutes.

If Kaffir lime leaves were not available, grate the rind of the remaining limes and add it to the pot. Juice the limes. Chop the green onions and mince the peppers, discarding the seeds. Add the green onions, cilantro, peppers, juice from the limes, fish sauce and coconut milk. Bring to a boil, remove from heat, and serve.

Beef Pho with Matsutake

This soup is also excellent with any edible species of Agaricus, especially the prince, or with shaggy mane, or with the stipes of boletes. We recommend making the broth the day before serving the soup, as it is a lengthy process. Excess broth may be frozen in quart batches, and used to make soup later.

Makes 1½ gallons of broth, soup on per serving basis.

Vietnamese Beef Broth

5 to 6 pounds of meaty beef knuckles or leg bones

1½ gallons cold water

2 medium onions

3-inch piece of fresh ginger

light-flavored vegetable oil

2 cinnamon sticks

1 tablespoon coriander seeds

1 tablespoon fennel seeds

4 star anise

6 whole cloves

1 black cardamom pod, if available

¼ cup dried candy caps (optional)

½ cup turkey tails or *Ganoderma* sp. (optional)

1½ tablespoons salt

¼ cup fish sauce

¼ cup rice vinegar or lime juice

2 tablespoons light brown sugar

To make a clear broth, put the beef bones in a large pot and cover with water. Bring to a boil; simmer 5 minutes. Drain off the water, discarding or saving for another purpose. Wash the pot and bones. This will get rid of most of the scum that often forms. Replace the bones in the pot, and fill with 6 quarts of water. Bring to a boil and turn down to a simmer. Lid the pot.

Do not peel the onions, just quarter them. Brush them with oil. Cut the ginger in half lengthwise, and brush it with oil. Char the onions and ginger under the broiler, on a grill or barbeque, or in a lightly oiled frying pan. Add them to the stock pot.

Toast the cinnamon sticks, coriander seeds, fennel seeds, star anise, cloves and black cardamom in a dry frying pan until they become fragrant. Place the candy caps, turkey tails or *Ganoderma*, and toasted spices in a muslin or cheesecloth bag and add it to the stock pot. Add the salt, fish sauce, vinegar or lime juice and sugar to the pot. Simmer for 3 to 6 hours, adding more water if necessary to keep the broth at the same level.

When the broth is done, remove the spice bag and strain out the other solids. Pick the meat out and reserve. If any meat is still clinging to the bones, pick it off and reserve it also. Skim the fat off with a spoon or allow to cool and refrigerate overnight, and lift off the hardened fat. Reserve 2 cups broth and 2 tablespoons boiled beef per serving, and freeze the rest for later use.

Pho Soup

Multiply these quantities by the number of servings you wish.

Makes 1 serving
1 ounce raw sirloin, rib-eye or tri-tip steak
2 cups broth from the recipe above
½ cup bean sprouts
1 sprig of fresh spearmint, garden mint or Moroccan mint
1 sprig of Thai basil
several slices of thinly sliced serrano or Thai bird chili pepper
1 wedge of lime
fish sauce, to taste
Hoisin sauce, to taste
Sriracha chili sauce, to taste

¼ to ½ pound fresh or half that weight dried ⅛-inch wide "banh pho" or rice noodles

2 tablespoons boiled beef, from the recipe above

8 to 12 very thin slices of matsutake

1 teaspoon sliced green onions

1 teaspoon chopped cilantro leaves

To make the soup, put the raw beef in the freezer for about ½ hour ahead of time to partially freeze it. Put on a pot of water to heat for the noodles. Put the required amount of broth into a pot over medium-high heat, and bring it to a boil.

Meanwhile, prepare serving dishes with bean sprouts, herbs, chilis and lime, and place them on the table along with the bottles of fish sauce, hoisin and sriracha.

Remove the beef from freezer and slice very thinly with a sharp knife.

When the water for the noodles comes to a boil, cook the noodles according to the instructions on the package.

Put the reserved boiled meat in a large strainer, and heat it by lowering it into the boiling broth for a few minutes.

Prepare the bowls, placing a portion of hot, cooked noodles in the bottom of each bowl. Then arrange the boiled beef, the raw beef and the matsutake or other mushroom slices on top. Ladle the simmering broth over these. Garnish with the green onion and cilantro. Guests top their own bowls with the assorted toppings.

Chicken Pho with Matsutake

Makes 1½ gallons of broth, so extra may be frozen.

If matsutakes are not available, this soup is also excellent with shaggy manes, deer mushrooms, volvariellas, meadow waxy cap, chanterelles or black trumpets. If using chanterelles, sauté them before putting them in the bowls.

Vietnamese Chicken Broth

1 chicken, excess fat removed

3 pounds chicken backs, necks, or other bony chicken parts

6 quarts water

2 yellow onions

4-inch section fresh ginger

light flavored vegetable oil

2 tablespoons coriander seeds

2 cinnamon sticks

2 star anise

4 green cardamom

¼ cup dried candy caps (optional)

½ cup turkey tails (optional)

1 small or ½ large bunch cilantro(save a little for garnish)

2 tablespoons salt

¼ cup lime juice or rice vinegar

¼ cup fish sauce

2 tablespoons light brown sugar

To make a clear broth, put the whole chicken and the chicken parts in a large pot and cover with water. (If organs came with the chicken, they may be reserved raw, for the soup, or they may be used for another purpose.) Bring the pot to a boil; simmer 5 minutes. Drain off the water, discarding or saving for another purpose. Wash the pot and the chicken. This will get rid of most of the scum that often forms. Replace the chicken in the pot, and fill with 6 quarts of water. Bring to a boil and turn down to a simmer. Lid the pot. Boil for 30 minutes; remove the whole chicken. Cut off the whole legs with thighs, and the breast meat, and set it aside. Refrigerate them after they cool, removing them from the refrigerator ½ hour before the soup is to be served. Return the rest of the chicken to the pot.

While the whole chicken boils, char the vegetables. Do not peel the onions, just quarter them. Brush them with oil. Cut the ginger in half lengthwise, and brush it with oil. Char the onions and ginger under the broiler, on a grill or barbeque, or in a lightly oiled frying pan. After the chicken meat has been removed, add them to the stock pot.

Toast the cinnamon sticks, coriander seeds, star anise and cardamom in a dry frying pan until they become fragrant. Place the candy caps, turkey tails, and toasted spices in a muslin or cheesecloth bag and add it to the stock pot. Tie the cilantro into a bunch with cotton string (removing any rubber band or wire tie), and toss it into the pot. Add the salt, fish sauce, vinegar or lime juice and sugar to the pot. Simmer for 3 to 6 hours, adding more water if necessary to keep the broth at the same level.

When the broth is done, remove the cilantro bunch and the spice bag, and strain out the solids. Skim the fat off with a spoon or allow to cool and refrigerate overnight, and lift off the hardened fat. Reserve 2 cups broth and ½ cup light and dark reserved chicken meat per desired serving, and freeze the rest for later use.

Pho Chicken Soup

Multiply these quantities by the number of servings you wish.

Makes 1 serving
2 cups broth from the above recipe
½ cup bean sprouts
1 sprig of fresh spearmint, garden mint or Moroccan mint
1 sprig of Thai basil
several slices of thinly sliced serrano or Thai bird chili pepper
1 wedge of lime
fish sauce, to taste
Hoisin sauce, to taste
Sriracha chili sauce, to taste
¼ to ½ pound fresh or half that weight dried ⅛-inch wide "banh pho" or rice noodles

½ cup thinly sliced cooked chicken, light and dark meat, from above recipe

a few slices of chicken organ meat (optional)

8 to 12 very thin slices of matsutake

1 teaspoon sliced green onions

1 teaspoon chopped cilantro leaves

If using chicken organs, put them in the freezer for ½ hour.

To make the soup, put on a pot of water to heat for the noodles. Put the required amount of broth into a pot over medium-high heat, and bring it to a boil.

Meanwhile, prepare serving dishes with bean sprouts, herbs, chilies and lime, and place them on the table along with the bottles of fish sauce, hoisin and sriracha.

Bone the reserved chicken, and slice the meat thinly. If using the organs, remove them from the freezer and slice them thinly.

When the water for the noodles comes to a boil, cook the noodles according to the instructions on the package.

Put the reserved chicken in a large strainer, and heat it by lowering it into the boiling broth for a few minutes.

Prepare the bowls, placing a portion of hot, cooked noodles in the bottom of each bowl. Then arrange the chicken, the raw organ meat and the matsutake or other mushroom slices on top. Ladle the simmering broth over these. Garnish with the green onion and cilantro. Guests top their own bowls with the assorted toppings.

Salads and Salad Dressings

Princely Green Salad

Any green salad is fit for a prince if you thinly slice an Agaricus augustus button and add it raw to the salad. If you have not eaten this mushroom raw before, observe the precautions used in trying out any new mushroom, as mushrooms are more difficult to digest raw than cooked. The flavor and texture of this mushroom raw greatly enhances a green salad.

Boletus Mirabilis Salad

Serves 4 to 6

8 large lettuce leaves

Stem of 1 large *Boletus mirabilis*

1 teaspoon butter

1 avocado

¼ red bell pepper

2 tablespoons olive oil

1 tablespoon soy sauce

1 tablespoon lemon juice

Slice the boletus very thinly and cut into bite sized pieces. Sauté in butter over medium heat until it begins to brown. Cool.

Tear lettuce leaves into salad bowl. Dice the avocado and add. Cut the bell pepper into bite sized slivers and add it, along with the mushrooms. Dress with olive oil, soy sauce, and lemon juice.

Toss and serve.

Matsutake Salad

Recipe inspired by Ryane Snow.

Serves 2 to 4

6 large lettuce leaves

1 cup bean sprouts

1 large Satsuma mandarin, preferably organic

¼ cup very thinly sliced raw matsutake

1 teaspoon minced fresh ginger

1 small clove of garlic, pressed

2 tablespoons mild-flavored oil such as peanut or sunflower

1 tablespoon soy sauce

1 tablespoon rice vinegar

1 teaspoon sugar or agave syrup (optional)

Tear the lettuce leaves into a salad bowl. Add the bean sprouts and matsutake. Peel mandarin (reserving a 2-inch square section of the peel), divide into sections, and cut each section in half and add to salad. Mince the reserved peel, and add to the salad along with the minced ginger and pressed garlic.

In a small cup, bowl or jar, combine the oil, soy sauce, vinegar and sugar. Whisk together or shake in a jar, dress the salad and serve immediately.

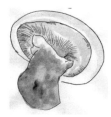

Salmon and Matsutake Oriental Salad

Serves 4

1 fully open matsutake

1 (4 to 6-ounce) salmon fillet, with skin if possible

2 teaspoons butter

3 cups shredded Napa cabbage

2 green onions, thinly sliced

¼ cup cilantro minced

1 small carrot, grated

1 tablespoon toasted sesame seeds

1 tablespoon peanut, walnut, or olive oil

½ teaspoon toasted sesame oil

1 tablespoon soy sauce

grated rind and juice from one lime

1 clove garlic, minced, mashed or pressed

½ teaspoon grated fresh ginger (or ¼ teaspoon powdered dried ginger)

¼ teaspoon red chili flakes (optional)

If the salmon fillet has skin (make sure it has been descaled), remove it and cut into julienne. Melt the butter in a skillet and fry the salmon skin until crispy. Remove it from the pan and set aside. Slice the matsutake thinly and put in the skillet. Put the salmon filet in the skillet also, on top of the mushrooms. Cook, covered, over low heat for 3 minutes. Turn salmon over, leaving the mushrooms on the bottom. As soon as salmon is cooked enough to flake with a fork, remove it from the pan. Leave the lid off the pan and continue cooking the mushrooms, stirring occasionally, until the water has evaporated. Allow to cool.

Combine cabbage, onions, cilantro and carrots in a small bowl. Flake the salmon over the salad, and add the mushrooms. Dress with the oils, soy sauce, lime juice and grated rind, ginger, garlic, chili and sesame seeds. Toss and serve. Garnish with crispy salmon skin.

Candy Cap Carrot Salad

A delicious twist on carrot-raisin salad!

Serves 8 to 12

5 carrots

½ orange or ½ cup pineapple

1 small apple

2 tablespoons raisins

2 tablespoons shredded coconut (optional)

2 tablespoons candy cap syrup (see recipe on page 219)

¼ cup mayonnaise

2 teaspoons lemon juice

Grate the carrots. Peel and chop the orange or pineapple. Core and chop the apple. Combine all ingredients in a bowl and mix well.

Porcini Panzanella

This salad may be served in a bread bowl. Use a round sour dough loaf, cut off the top, and hollow out to create a bowl, using ½ of the bread you removed to cut into cubes for the recipe. Make the salad in a bowl and transfer it into the crust just before serving.

Serves 4

½ loaf stale sourdough bread

2 tablespoons butter

1 pound ripe tomatoes

¼ cup olive oil

2 tablespoons red wine vinegar

½ teaspoon salt

½ cup grated Parmesan cheese

¼ cup dried porcini

1 yellow or red bell pepper

1 jalapeno pepper

2 cloves garlic

½ cup pitted kalamata olives

2 tablespoons capers

2 anchovy filets

1 bunch basil

Cut the bread into cubes. Toast them in a frying pan in the butter.

Chop the tomatoes and put them with their juices into a salad bowl with the oil, vinegar, and salt. Tear or cut the dried mushrooms into the bowl. Smash the tomatoes somewhat to squeeze the juices out. Add the bread and toss.

Dice the bell pepper, mince the jalapeno and garlic and add them to the salad. (If desired, you may roast and peel the peppers first). Coarsely chop the olives and add them, along with the capers. Mince the anchovies and add. Tear the basil and add, and add the Parmesan cheese. Toss, let marinate for about 1 hour and serve.

Princely Potato-Fennel Salad

Serves 4

2 large potatoes

1 bulb fennel

1 large *Agaricus augustus* (about 2 cups, chopped)

2 tablespoons butter

2 stalks celery, minced

2 tablespoons fresh chives, minced, or ¼ cup chopped green onion

1 teaspoon minced fresh parsley or chervil

1 teaspoon tarragon, fresh if available

3 tablespoons vegetable oil or mayonnaise

2 tablespoons lemon juice or wine vinegar, or to taste

Salt to taste

Boil the potatoes, preferably whole, allow to cool, then dice. Put them into a bowl. (If in a hurry, you can dice them first, but you loose more starch in the water.)

Meanwhile, slice the fennel bulb and sauté it in 1 tablespoon of the butter. Add it to the bowl. Chop and sauté the mushroom in the remaining tablespoon of butter, and add it to the bowl. Add the celery, chives or onion, tarragon and parsley. Dress with oil or mayonnaise and lemon juice or vinegar and salt to taste.

Boletus Salad

This salad may be made with rice, buckwheat groats, quinoa, pasta or other grain.

Serves 8

1 cup dried boletus, chopped

1 cup pasta or grain

1 carrot, diced

½ cup grated zucchini

1 red bell pepper

2 stalks celery

2 cups bean or lentil sprouts

2 green onions, thinly sliced

½ cup chopped kale

⅓ cup olive oil

¼ cup lemon juice

½ teaspoon red pepper flakes (optional)

¼ cup roasted, salted, shelled pumpkin seeds

2 sprigs parsley, chopped

¼ teaspoon minced fresh rosemary

¼ teaspoon oregano, fresh or dried

1 cup chopped tomato

3 to 4 sprigs fresh basil

2 tablespoons red wine vinegar

½ teaspoon salt, or to taste

Put the dried mushrooms and carrots in a saucepan. Add water to just cover. Bring to a boil and remove from heat and allow to soak for 10 minutes. Drain off and reserve liquid. Cook the grain according to its requirements, using the reserved mushroom soaking water as part of the required water.

While the grain is cooking, cut the bell pepper into slivers and slice the celery and onions thinly. Rub the chopped kale between your hands to bruise and soften it. Put red pepper, onion, kale, celery, mushrooms and carrots in a large bowl. Add the sprouts, zucchini, pumpkin seeds, parsley, rosemary, oregano, and red pepper flakes.

In a small bowl, tear the basil leaves into the chopped tomatoes and set aside.

When the grain is done, remove from heat and allow it to cool for 10 minutes. Add it to the large bowl, and stir it in. Dress with olive oil, vinegar, lemon juice and salt, and allow to cool completely. Toss in the tomatoes and basil and chill before serving.

White Bean, Tomato, and Chanterelle Salad

Serves 2 to 4

1¼ cup cooked white beans (or one can, drained)

1 cup chopped tomatoes, or quartered cherry tomatoes

¼ cup finely chopped onion

2 cloves garlic, minced or pressed

½ teaspoon minced fresh rosemary leaves

2 cups chopped chanterelles

2 tablespoons olive oil

1 tablespoon balsamic vinegar

½ teaspoon salt

¼ cup grated Parmesan cheese

12 fresh basil leaves, torn up

Dry sauté the chanterelles until they give up their moisture and it mostly evaporates. If using early season "dry" chanterelles, sauté them in a tablespoon of butter or oil. Combine with all other ingredients, toss, chill, and serve.

Couscous, Beansprout and Morel Salad

You may use fresh morels in this dish rather than the dried called for, but clean and sauté them well in a little olive oil, then add them after the couscous or quinoa has been cooked. They will give a more delicate flavor than the dried. Use about 1 cup fresh morels.

Serves 4

½ cup dried morels, quartered

½ cup couscous or quinoa

½ cup shelled green peas or snow or snap peas cut into bite-sized pieces

1 ear of corn or ½ cup frozen corn kernels

2 tablespoons olive oil

1 cup bean sprouts

2 green onions, chopped

½ red bell pepper, chopped (optional)

1 carrot, coarsely grated or slivered or julienned

2 tablespoons minced parsley

1 tablespoon lemon juice

½ teaspoon salt

½ teaspoon fresh minced spearmint

½ teaspoon tarragon or 1 teaspoon fresh minced tarragon

1 clove garlic, minced

In a lidded sauce pan, bring 1 cup of water and the morels to a boil.

Meanwhile, if using couscous, toast it in a dry frying pan, stirring often, until the pearls are light brown. If using quinoa, put it in a strainer and rinse it well under running water. When the water with the morels is boiling, add the couscous or quinoa to it. When the water returns to a boil, turn it down to a simmer, replacing the lid.

If using fresh corn, cut the kernels from the ear. Prepare the peas. After the couscous has been boiling 9 minutes or the quinoa 12, add the peas and corn to the pot. Replace the lid and boil 3 more minutes. Remove from heat. Let sit for 3 more minutes.

Turn the cooked mixture out into a salad bowl. Dress immediately with olive oil, tossing to coat the kernels. Prepare the other vegetables and add them, then toss in the lemon juice, salt, garlic and herbs. Chill before serving.

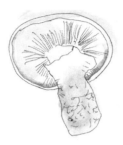

3-Bean Salad with Matsutake and Corn

May be made several days in advance and flavors will mingle.

Serves 6 to 8

1¼ cups kidney beans, cooked or 1 (14-ounce) can

1¼ cups garbanzo beans cooked, or 1 (14-ounce) can

1 cup cooked green beans, cut into 1-inch pieces (may use frozen or canned)

1 cup cooked corn kernels (may use frozen or canned)

½ cup red onion, finely chopped

2 (4 to 5-inch diameter) open matsutakes, chopped

2 tablespoons olive oil

2 tablespoons rice vinegar

2 teaspoons soy sauce

Sauté the matsutakes and onions in the oil. Place in a salad bowl. If using any frozen vegetables, cook according to instructions on the package, drain, and add. If using any canned ingredients, drain them and add to the bowl. Add all other ingredients, toss, chill, and serve.

Curried Egg Salad with Chanterelles or Hedgehogs

Serves 4

1 cup chopped chanterelles or hedgehogs

1 tablespoon butter, or olive or coconut oil

8 hard-boiled eggs

2 stalks celery, minced

1 tablespoon minced onion

½ red bell pepper, minced

¼ cup mayonnaise

1 teaspoon curry powder, or to taste

1 tablespoon rice vinegar

½ teaspoon salt, or to taste

Sauté the mushrooms in the butter or oil, then allow them to cool. Peel and chop the eggs, and put them into a bowl. Add the mushrooms and all other ingredients. Stir, chill and serve as a side dish, topping for a vegetable salad or as a sandwich spread.

Egg Salad with Green Olives and Yellow Feet or Porcini

Serves 4 to 6

1 cup chopped yellow feet or ¼ cup dried porcini

1 tablespoon olive oil (not needed if using porcini)

8 hard boiled eggs

12 pimento-stuffed green olives

1 tablespoon minced onion

¼ cup mayonnaise

1 tablespoon brine from the olives

Salt to taste

Sauté the yellow feet in oil until they soften, or snip Porcini into small pieces with kitchen shears, put them in a small bowl and cover them with boiling water, allowing them to soak 15 minutes, then drain, saving liquid, if desired, for another purpose.

Peel and chop the eggs, putting them into a bowl. Add the mushrooms. Slice the olives crosswise into ⅛ inch thick slices, and add. Add all other ingredients. Serve as a side dish, as a topping to a green salad or as a sandwich spread.

Chanterelle and Shrimp Aspic (Clear)

Serves 10 to 12
3 cups chicken broth
2 tablespoons gelatin
1 cup chanterelles, chopped
2 teaspoons butter or olive oil
½ cup celery
3 cloves garlic, minced
½ cup salad shrimp
1 medium tomato
1 tablespoon soy sauce
1 tablespoon lemon juice
1 tablespoon capers

Put the broth in a saucepan. Sprinkle the gelatin on the surface and let it sit 5 minutes to soften. Meanwhile, sauté the chanterelles in oil until their liquid has mostly evaporated. When nearly done, add garlic and sauté a few more minutes.

Heat the broth until quite warm and gelatin dissolves completely. Do not boil. Remove from heat, allow to cool to lukewarm. Chop the celery and tomato. Combine all ingredients, pour into a 6-cup Jello mold or metal bowl, and refrigerate 1½ to 2 hours or until it thickens. Stir, and chill 2 more hours, until set. See recipe on page 118 for unmolding instructions.

Tomato, Shrimp and Hedgehog Aspic

This is also excellent with chanterelles or black trumpets. Fistulina hepatica *can be used — the tart taste goes with the tomato, but use only 1 cup. It's also good with dried* Boletus *mushrooms — use only ½ cup dried* Boletus, *and soak it in 1½ cup hot water until the water has cooled. Then drain, measuring out ½ cup of the water. Dissolve the gelatin in this, and proceed with the recipe. Mince the drained dried mushrooms, and add them along with the other vegetables, no need to stir-fry them.*

Serves 10 to 12

2 packets or 2 tablespoons unflavored gelatin

2 cups hedgehog mushrooms

1 teaspoon butter

½ teaspoon red or white miso

½ teaspoon prepared horseradish

2½ cups tomato, V-8, or spicy-hot tomato juice

¼ cup finely minced onion

¼ cup finely minced celery

½ cup chopped cress, arugula, mizuma, grated radish or tender mustard greens

1 cup salad shrimp

Put ½ cup of water in a small saucepan, and sprinkle the gelatin over it. Allow to sit for 5 minutes. Then heat the gelatin over low heat, stirring, until it has dissolved, then remove from heat immediately. Do not boil. Stir the miso and horseradish in to 2 tablespoons of the tomato juice, until the lumps are gone. Add the rest of the tomato juice and the miso mixture to the gelatin in a bowl and stir thoroughly. Allow to cool, then chill for 1½ to 2 hours, until it just begins to thicken, but has not gelled fully.

Meanwhile, clean and chop the mushrooms, and sauté in butter until they release their water and the water has evaporated, and the mushrooms begin to brown, slightly. Cool.

When the gelatin is ready, stir in the mushrooms and all remaining ingredients. Pour into a 6-cup Jello mold. Chill until set—another 2 hours or overnight.

When ready to serve, fill the sink halfway with hot water from the tap, and hold the mold in it to just below the rim for 20 seconds if using a metal mold. (If using a glass or ceramic bowl as a mold, it may take a little longer—try 40 seconds). Remove from the water bath, lay a plate upside down over the mold and invert onto the plate. If the aspic is still stuck tightly to the mold, repeat this process. If it almost comes out, but is just a little stuck, wet a dishtowel in hot water, wring out, and wrap the stuck area of the mold with it until the aspic pops out.

Beet and Black Trumpet Aspic

Yellow feet, chanterelles or hedgehogs may be substituted.

12 to 15 servings
1¾ cups raw julienned beets, (or one can julienned beets with liquid)
2 tablespoons unflavored gelatin (2 packages)
1 cup black trumpets
1 teaspoon butter or light flavored oil
Scant ¼ cup sugar, or to taste
Juice of one lemon
⅜ cup rice vinegar
½ teaspoon salt
Pinch of cloves
Pinch of nutmeg
Sour cream for garnish

Boil the beets in 1½ cups water until they are tender. If using canned beets, omit this step. Either way, reserve the beet liquid.

Soften the gelatin for 5 minutes in one cup of cold water in a small saucepan. Meanwhile, sauté the mushrooms in the butter or oil until just done.

Heat the gelatin and water slowly, stirring until the gelatin dissolves; remove from heat. Stir in the mushrooms and their cooking liquid. Add the sugar, lemon juice, vinegar, salt, and spices. Add the beets and beet juice and enough cold water to make 4½ to 5 cups. This looks nice in an 8-inch square glass baking dish or other shallow glass dish. Pour into dish, or if preferred, a Jello mold, and chill until set. (See recipe on page 118 for unmolding instructions if you use a mold.) Serve with sour cream garnish.

Raw Cocorra Slaw

This is best if the salad dressing is made several days in advance.

Serves 6
2 cup shredded cabbage
½ cup grated kohlrabi, or peeled, grated broccoli stem
2 leaves kale
2 tablespoons minced onion
¼ cup thinly sliced celery
½ small cucumber, quartered and sliced
2 calendula flowers (if available)
1 cup thinly sliced *Amanita calyptoderma*.

Combine cabbage, kohlrabi, onion, celery, cucumber and mushroom. Remove the ribs from the kale leaves and thinly slice them. Roll and rub the leaves between your hands to soften them. Add to salad. Pick petals from calendula flowers and add to the salad. Dress with garlic-porcini vinaigrette. (See recipe below.)

Garlic-Porcini Vinaigrette

Makes about 1¼ cup cup
⅔ cup olive oil
⅓ cup wine vinegar or rice vinegar
3 tablespoons soy sauce
2 cloves garlic, minced
½ teaspoon minced thyme
1 tablespoon ground dried porcini

Combine and allow to mellow in the refrigerator for two or three days to marry the flavors before using. If you wish to use it immediately, purée it in a blender to extract the flavors.

Mushroom Vinaigrette

Makes ¾ cup

½ cup olive oil

¼ cup red wine vinegar

1 to 2 teaspoons mushroom salt (see recipe on page 256)

1 small clove garlic, pressed

½ teaspoon dried basil

¼ teaspoon thyme

¼ teaspoon tarragon (optional)

Place all ingredients in a jar and shake well to blend.

Mushroom Soy Vinaigrette

Makes about 1 cup

½ cup olive oil

¼ cup rice vinegar

¼ cup soy sauce

½ teaspoon toasted sesame oil

1 tablespoon ground dried matsutake or Porcini or ¼ cup fresh minced matsutake

½ teaspoon thyme

½ teaspoon tarragon

½ teaspoon powdered ginger

1 small clove garlic, pressed

Put all ingredients in a jar and shake well to blend or mix in blender until smooth. Best if made a day in advance of using, to allow flavors to meld.

Lemon Mushroom Salad Dressing

Makes about 1 cup

⅔ cup olive oil

Juice and grated rind from one lemon

¼ teaspoon salt

1 tablespoon dried ground *Boletus mirabilis* or porcini

1 teaspoon lemon thyme

1 teaspoon lemon balm (if available)

1 small clove garlic, pressed

Put all ingredients in a jar and shake to mix well, or purée in a blender for a smooth dressing.

Candy Cap Fruit Salad Dressing

Makes about 1 cup

½ cup yogurt

½ cup sour cream

2 tablespoons candy cap syrup (see recipe on page 219)

1 teaspoon lemon juice

½ teaspoon cinnamon

¼ teaspoon powdered ginger

Pinch of nutmeg

Stir all ingredients together. Use to dress fruit salad. Will keep for two weeks in the refrigerator.

Sandwiches

Bacon, Lettuce, Tomato and Mushroom Sandwich

This recipe may be made with Agaricus augustus, *early chanterelles, or dried porcini, or any other mushroom that's up while the tomatoes are ripe.*

Serves 1
1 slice bacon
Mushroom slices
2 slices bread
Mayonnaise
1 large slice tomato
1 leaf lettuce

Cut the bacon slice in half, into 2 shorter slices. Fry them until they are crisp and set aside.

If using fresh mushrooms, fry them in a little of the bacon grease or in butter until they are cooked through. If using dried mushrooms, soak them in a little boiling water until they are rehydrated. Simmer until they are soft and all the liquid has evaporated.

Toast the bread, lightly. Spread both slices with mayonnaise. Assemble the bacon, mushroom, tomato and lettuce on one slice and top with the second slice.

Brandied Mushrooms on Toast

This recipe is reprinted from Gathered Mushroom Recipes, *a collection of recipes by Teresa Sholars' 1981 mushroom class at the Mendocino Coast Branch of College of the Redwoods.*

Serves 1

1 medium wild mushroom, about 1 cup sliced or chopped

1 small clove garlic, minced

Pinch of oregano

1 teaspoon butter

1 slice bread

½ teaspoon brandy

½ teaspoon grated Parmesan cheese

Sauté the mushroom, garlic and oregano in butter until the mushroom is done. Meanwhile, toast the bread, and preheat the broiler. Stir the brandy into the mushrooms, and heap them onto the toast. Sprinkle with Parmesan cheese, and put under the broiler for a few minutes before serving.

Matsutake Burgers

The matsutakes in this recipe may be marinated overnight or longer; if marinated the same day as cooking, allow at least ½ hour to marinate.

Serves 4

1 cup marinated matsutakes (see recipe on page 52)

1 small onion, sliced

1 pound hamburger, 80% lean

4 hamburger buns

mayonnaise

hoisin sauce

1 cup bean sprouts or sliced Chinese cabbage

Marinate the matsutakes at least ½ hour in advance. Sauté the matsutakes and onions together. When the mushrooms and onions are partially cooked, form the hamburger into 4 patties and, in a second pan, sauté them to desired doneness. Warm the buns. Spread mayonnaise and hoisin sauce on the buns, and fill the sandwich with a burger patty, mushrooms and onions, and bean sprouts or Chinese cabbage.

Boletus Burger

This can be made with dried boletus: barely cover the dried mushrooms with boiling water, let sit until soft, then simmer until the water has boiled off.

Serves 4
Fresh boletus slices
2 cloves garlic, minced
1 tablespoon olive oil
4 slices onion
1 pound hamburger (or a little more if you like big burgers)
8 oil-packed sun-dried tomato halves
4 hamburger buns or 8 slices bread
Mayonnaise
Ketchup
Parmesan cheese
4 leaves lettuce

In a large frying pan over medium-high heat, sauté the mushroom slices with the garlic in the olive oil, turning to cook both sides. Set them aside, and in the same pan, sauté the onion until it is golden. Set aside the onion, and put the buns on to warm on a large griddle, or in the oven. Turn the heat down under the skillet to medium, and form the meat into 4 patties. Sauté the hamburgers to the doneness you prefer.

Assemble the hamburgers: spread mayonnaise and ketchup on the buns, put on the burgers, mushroom, onion, 2 sun-dried tomato halves, each cut in half, sprinkle with Parmesan cheese, and top with lettuce and the tops of the buns.

Peanut Butter and Candy Cap Sandwich

Serves 1

2 slices bread

Butter (optional)

1 to 2 tablespoons peanut butter

1 tablespoon candy cap honey (see recipe on page 220)

Bread may be toasted if desired. Spread one slice of the bread with butter, then peanut butter. If desired, you may brown the peanut butter under a broiler, watching carefully, until it bubbles. Spread the other slice of bread with butter, then candy cap honey. Put the two pieces together into a sandwich.

Mushroom Quesadillas

Chopped mushrooms

Grated cheese

Tortillas

Salsa

Avocado (optional)

Cilantro

For each quesadilla sauté ¼ to ½ cup mushrooms. Place a tortilla in an ungreased frying pan over medium heat. Warm on one side, flip, sprinkle on a good handful of cheese; add mushrooms and salsa, and fold in half. Turn over when cheese starts to melt.

Remove from heat when both sides are done and serve with sliced avocado, chopped cilantro, and more salsa to taste.

Side Dishes

Ryane Snow's Mushroom Bacon

Recipe by Ryane Snow. Ryane used golden or white chanterelles for this recipe. It is also good using smoked pig's ears (see recipe on page 255 for smoking mushrooms).

Chanterelles
Salt or smoked mushroom salt (see recipe on page 256)
Olive oil

Preheat the oven to 250° F. Tear the chanterelles by starting at the edge of the cap and separating them with your fingers into long strips. You'll have a pile of neat chanterelle curls. Toss them with olive oil, salt liberally, spread thinly onto a baking sheet, and bake about an hour, until crispy, stirring every once in awhile to prevent sticking or burning.

For additional flavoring you can sprinkle with smoked paprika or with smoky mushroom powder. (See directions on page 255)

Baked Matsutake

Serves 6 to 8

2 large matsutake mushrooms, sliced thinly, about a pint
1 large leek, white parts only, sliced
2 tablespoons rice wine vinegar
2 tablespoons tamari (soy sauce)
½ cup mirin (cooking sake)

Preheat the oven to 400° F. Mix all ingredients and place in a 9 by 13-inch glass baking dish. Bake until liquid is absorbed and leeks and mushrooms both get caramelized and crispy, about an hour.

Sweet and Sour Matsutake

This recipe is reprinted from Gathered Mushroom Recipes, *a booklet by Teresa Sholars' fall 1981 mushroom class at the Fort Bragg branch of College of the Redwoods.*

Serves 4

2 to 4 matsutakes

½ cup pineapple juice

¼ cup rice vinegar

3 tablespoons peanut or coconut oil

2 tablespoons brown sugar

1 teaspoon cornstarch

¼ teaspoon pepper

Preheat oven to 350° F. Slice the matsutakes ¼ inch thick and lay them in a single layer on a baking sheet. Bake them for 20 minutes.

Combine all remaining ingredients in a small saucepan. Heat to a simmer over medium-low heat, stirring constantly, until it thickens slightly. Divide into 4 small bowls. Serve the matsutakes with this dipping sauce.

Mulled Chanterelles

Inspired by Ryane Snowe. This dish can be made as a side dish or vegetarian entrée without the pork, or used as an accompaniment to pork chops or roast pork.

Serves 4

2 tablespoons butter

½ onion, sliced

2 cups chopped chanterelles

½ pound pork, sliced thinly

2 apples, cored and chopped

½ cup sweet red wine

½ teaspoon salt or to taste

½ teaspoon cinnamon

½ teaspoon ground coriander

Pinch of nutmeg

¼ teaspoon thyme

½ cup huckleberries (optional)

½ teaspoon cornstarch

Melt the butter in a frying pan and sauté the onions until they begin to brown. Add the chanterelles, and sauté until they exude their liquid. Add the pork, apple, wine, salt and spices; cover and cook for 5 to 10 minutes, until the pork and apple are cooked.

Remove the pork, apple and mushrooms from the pan to a serving bowl with a slotted spoon, and stir the huckleberries into the mushroom blend, if using. Replace the frying pan with the juices onto the burner. Mix the cornstarch in 2 tablespoons of water, then stir this mixture into the simmering juices. When thickened, pour the sauce over the mushroom mixture, stir in, and serve.

Hedgehogs Sauté

Serves 2

2 tablespoons butter

1 tablespoon oil (coconut, sesame, olive)

1 medium shallot, sliced

1 cup sliced hedgehogs

3 garlic cloves, chopped

1 cup sliced Napa cabbage

¼ cup chopped parsley

Dash brown rice vinegar

Dash tamari

Smoky Porcini salt (see recipe on page 256)

Black pepper and salt to taste

Melt butter with oil over medium heat, in a skillet. Add shallots and mushrooms and sauté until nearly done, stirring frequently. Add chopped garlic, Napa cabbage and parsley and stir-fry a few minutes. Splash on the vinegar, tamari. Season with a little bit of porcini salt. Then add salt and pepper to taste. Remove from heat and serve while the cabbage retains a little bit of crunchiness. Makes a perfect side dish or garnish for mashed potatoes, or rice.

Black and White Sauté

Hedgehogs and black trumpets.

Serves 2 to 3

2 tablespoons butter

1 tablespoon olive or avocado oil

1 shallot, sliced (optional)

2 cups sliced hedgehogs

1 cup black chanterelles, torn into strips

Chopped garlic to taste, about 2-3 cloves

3 tablespoons cooking sherry or rice vinegar

1 cup chopped parsley or cilantro

salt and pepper to taste

Melt the butter with the oil in a heavy skillet. Add the shallots and mushrooms and stir-fry for a few minutes, then add garlic and stir a few more times. Cook about 5 minutes on medium heat. When mushrooms are softened and half done, add the sherry and cook another 5 to 10 minutes.

Add the chopped parsley or cilantro, and continue to stir until all is well mixed. If liquid evaporates and mushrooms are still underdone, add more water, a little at a time, and continue to sauté. This dish can be cooked for as long as 20 minutes—the mushrooms just get more and more flavorful. Soy sauce or rice wine vinegar may also be added, to taste.

Mashed Potatoes with Leeks and Mushrooms

This is excellent with almost any mushroom. We'd recommend either golden, white or black chanterelles, or gamboni or other boletes, fresh or dried, or blewits, shaggy manes, man on horseback, sweetbread mushroom, milk caps, russulas, agaricus or matsutake.

Serves 6

3 large potatoes or 4 to 6 medium to small ones

1 cup thinly sliced leek, green portions included

2 cups finely chopped mushroom

2 tablespoons butter

½ teaspoon thyme

¼ cup sherry

¼ cup milk or half and half

1 teaspoon salt or to taste

pepper to taste

Dice and boil the potatoes, peeling first if desired. Meanwhile sauté the leeks and mushrooms in 1 tablespoon of the butter for 5 minutes. Add the thyme and sherry, cover and simmer 10 minutes. Uncover the mushrooms, and boil off the excess water until they are moist but not swimming.

When the potatoes are done, drain them and mash them with the remaining butter, milk and seasonings, stir in the mushroom mixture, and serve topped with gravy, butter or sour cream. Garnish with chives.

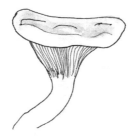

Princely Mashed Potatoes

The prince flavors the potatoes nicely in this simple recipe.

Serves 4

1 medium *Agaricus augustus*

2 large russet or 3 to 4 smaller red, white or yellow potatoes, peeled if desired

2 tablespoons butter

½ teaspoon salt or to taste

¼ cup half-and-half or milk

¼ cup sour cream

Mince the mushroom and sauté in a tablespoon of the butter until they are cooked through. Meanwhile, dice and boil the potatoes. When the potatoes are tender, drain off the liquid and add the remaining butter, salt, milk, and sour cream. Mash, stir in the mushrooms and serve with additional sour cream or gravy.

Dreamy Mashed Potatoes

The combination of bacon and mapley candy caps infuses this dish with flavor.

2 large red potatoes, peeled if desired

2 strips bacon

2 tablespoons minced onions

½ cup fresh candy cap mushrooms

2 cloves garlic, minced

¼ cup milk or half and half

1 tablespoon butter

½ teaspoon salt or to taste

Cut up potatoes, and put them into a saucepan with a little water. Boil them until tender.

Meanwhile, mince the bacon and sauté it in a frying pan. When the bacon is done, pour off the excess grease and spread the bacon on a paper towel to drain.

Sauté the onions in the remaining bacon grease in the pan, until golden and caramelized. Remove from pan to bowl. Turn the heat down to low. Then mince the candy caps and sauté them until just fragrant (be careful not to overcook them as they lose their flavor), adding a little more bacon grease to the pan, if necessary. Add them to the onions. Sauté the garlic until just fragrant, and add them to the onions, also.

Drain and mash the potatoes. Mix in the butter and milk, the bacon, onions, mushrooms and garlic. Salt to taste. Serve immediately, with extra butter or sour cream.

Potatoes on Horseback

Sweetbread mushroom, and any agaricus are also good cooked this way.

Serves 4 to 6

2 medium potatoes, thinly sliced

2 cups Man on Horseback mushrooms, sliced

½ cup green or red bell pepper, sliced

½ teaspoon salt

Butter or oil for frying

Sauté the potatoes in the oil or butter until nearly done. Add the mushrooms and sauté 5 minutes until slightly done. Add peppers and continue to cook until all are done to your satisfaction, about another 5 minutes on medium flame.

Suitable served as a side dish for breakfast or dinner.

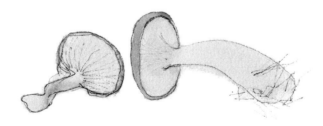

Mashed or Country-Fried Purple Potatoes with Blewits

This recipe is equally good with white or red potatoes. Purple potatoes may sometimes be found at farmers' markets and in some grocery stores that carry specialty vegetables, or perhaps you grow them yourself. When using purple-fleshed potatoes, do not cut or peel the potatoes before cooking them, as the intact skin prevents the water from bleaching out the color of the flesh. The two most common cultivars of purple-fleshed potatoes are Purple Peruvian Fingerlings and All-Blue (a full-sized potato). Purple Peruvians have a deeper color, and will come out a brighter purple; All-Blues come out lavender. For a color contrast, substitute milk caps for blewits.

Serves 4

3 to 4 full-sized purple potatoes or 2 to 3 cups of fingerlings

¼ red onion

2 large blewits

2 tablespoons butter

2 tablespoons milk (for mashed)

½ teaspoon salt or to taste

Pinch of nutmeg

Put the potatoes whole into a pot and cover them with water. Bring to a boil and simmer until barely tender for frying, or very tender for mashing. Meanwhile, finely chop the onions and mushrooms.

For fried potatoes: melt the butter in a skillet over moderate heat. As soon as the potatoes are barely tender, chop them and add them, with the mushrooms and onions, to the skillet. Add the salt and nutmeg, and sauté a few minutes until the potatoes are tender and the mushrooms and onions are cooked.

For mashed: sauté the mushrooms and onions in a skillet, in 1 tablespoon of the butter.

When the potatoes are completely tender, if you wish to peel them, allow them to cool enough to handle them, then peel and mash. If you wish to leave the peelings on, just mash them. Mix in the mushrooms and onions. Mix in the remaining butter, the milk, salt and nutmeg. If the potatoes have cooled, reheat in the oven or microwave before serving.

Russula Potato Melt

Serves 4

4 medium white potatoes

1 to 2 carrots

1 cup peas

½ onion

1 tablespoon butter

2 to 3 *Russula cyanthoxantha* or *R. xerampolina* (about 2 cups chopped)

½ cup grated cheddar or Swiss cheese

2 cloves garlic, minced or pressed

Salt and pepper to taste

Cut potatoes and carrots into chunks; steam until tender. Add peas and steam a few more minutes. Meanwhile, dice the onion and mushrooms and sauté in butter. Add the garlic when the mushrooms are done and sauté one minute more until the garlic is fragrant. Combine steamed vegetables in a large warm bowl with sautéed mushrooms and onions, stir in grated cheese, and salt and pepper, and cover until cheese melts.

Candy Cap Yams

This recipe has a more subtle flavor than the following one. The baked candy caps can afterward be used minced in another dish. These may also be baked in a barbeque, campfire, wood stove or fireplace, generally for a lesser time, as the temperature is hotter. Check yams for doneness by piercing with a knife.

yams

fresh candy caps

aluminum foil

Preheat the oven to 350° F. For each yam, tear off a sheet of aluminum foil large enough to wrap it completely.

Lay yam on foil. Lay a row of candy caps spaced about 1 inch apart on either side. Wrap the whole thing tightly and bake for about an hour (depending upon size of yam) or until soft through to center. Serve with butter.

Twice Baked Candy Cap Yams

Serves 8

2 to 3 medium sized yams—about 4 to 5 cups

½ cup minced fresh or 2 tablespoons ground dried candy caps

2 tablespoons butter

1 teaspoon cinnamon

½ teaspoon ginger (optional)

¼ teaspoon nutmeg or mace

½ cup raisins and/or crushed pineapple and/or chopped nuts (optional)

Preheat the oven to 350° F. Bake the yams whole until done, about one hour. Remove the yams, but leave the oven on.

Peel and mash the yams in a bowl. Mix in all other ingredients. Put in an 8-inch square baking dish and bake again for 20 minutes. Serve with butter.

Oyster Stuffed Mushrooms

This recipe is reprinted from Gathered Mushroom Recipes, *a booklet by Teresa Sholars' fall 1981 mushroom class at the Fort Bragg branch of College of the Redwoods. You may use oyster mushrooms for this, or any type with a flat cap.*

Makes about 10

1 jar medium-sized oysters

10 mushroom caps (about 3-inch diameter)

Butter for sautéing

Preheat broiler. Meanwhile, sauté the mushroom caps lightly on each side, in butter. Put the caps, gill sides up, on a baking sheet, and top each one with an oyster. Broil, watching until the oysters plump. Remove from broiler, and serve as a side dish or appetizer. May be served on slices of baguette or crackers, for finger food.

Creamed Chicken of the Woods

Be sure not to use Laetiporus *that was growing on Eucalyptus; those tend to be toxic.*

Serves 6 to 8

2 cups diced chicken of the woods

1 cup diced onion

2 cups peas, shelled green, or frozen

2 tablespoons butter

4 cloves garlic, minced

1 cup milk

1 cup half and half

2 tablespoons cornstarch

½ to 1 teaspoon salt, to taste

Par-boil the mushroom in water for 10 minutes. Drain. Sauté the onion and mushroom in butter until the onion is translucent. Add the garlic and peas, cover and cook for 3 minutes. Add the half and half, and ¾ cup of the milk, stirring frequently. Mix the cornstarch into the remaining ¼ cup milk, and add it when the mushroom mixture comes to a boil, stirring constantly until it thickens. Salt to taste. Serve over toast, rice or noodles.

Cheese Stuffed Mushrooms

This recipe is reprinted from Gathered Mushroom Recipes, *a booklet by Teresa Sholars' fall 1981 mushroom class at the Fort Bragg branch of College of the Redwoods.*

Makes 10

10 mushroom caps

Butter for sautéing

Cheese (amount depends on size of mushrooms) Brie, cheddar, Gouda, blue or Swiss

Preheat the broiler. Sauté the mushroom caps lightly on both sides in butter. Cut the cheese into pieces that will fit on the caps and give room to melt without running off. Place the mushrooms on a baking sheet, gill side up, and place the cheese on the mushrooms. Put them under the broiler, watching carefully. Broil until the cheese melts.

Depending on the size of the mushroom, this may be served as an appetizer, a side dish, or an entrée.

Stuffed Mushrooms

This recipe is reprinted from Gathered Mushroom Recipes, *a booklet by Teresa Sholars' fall 1981 mushroom class at the Fort Bragg branch of College of the Redwoods.*

Makes 10

10 (3-inch) mushrooms, with flat caps

Butter for sautéing

2 tablespoons minced onion

1 or 2 cloves garlic, minced

1 tablespoon minced parsley

½ cup bread crumbs

¼ cup grated jack cheese or softened cream cheese

2 tablespoons white wine

¼ teaspoon thyme

1 tablespoon Parmesan cheese

Cut the stems from the mushrooms and mince them. Sauté the mushroom caps lightly in butter on both sides, and put them, gill side up on a baking sheet. Sauté the minced mushroom stalks, onion, garlic and parsley in butter. Mix them with the bread crumbs in a small bowl. Stir in the cheese, wine, thyme and Parmesan.

Preheat the broiler. Put a spoonful of the filling on each mushroom cap. Broil until the cheese melts and the filling begins to brown.

Delicious Lactarius Rice

This can be made with any edible Lactarius *or* Russula. *The boiling with the rice helps soften the grainy texture of these mushrooms.*

Serves 4

1 cup rice

1 cup chopped *Lactarius deliciosus*

¼ cup chopped onion

1 clove garlic

¼ teaspoon cumin seeds

¼ cup chopped toasted almonds

Put the rice, mushroom, onion, garlic and cumin seeds in a saucepan. Add 2 cups water. Bring to a boil, cover and turn down to a simmer. Simmer for 30 to 45 minutes depending on the type of rice. Garnish with almonds, serve with butter and salt, or soy sauce.

Boletus Risotto

Serves 6

½ cup dried *Boletus edulis* (or other edible bolete), chopped

3 cups low salt broth or stock, chicken or vegetable

½ medium onion, chopped

2 tablespoons olive oil

¾ cup short grain white rice (arborio is the classic risotto rice type)

¼ cup Parmesan cheese, grated

Salt and pepper to taste

¼ cup chopped toasted almonds

Minced Italian parsley for garnish

Heat the broth to low simmer. Meanwhile, in a separate 6 to 8-cup saucepan, melt the butter over medium to low heat and sauté the onions and mushrooms until tender.

Add the rice and sauté, stirring constantly, until the rice has begun to toast very slightly. Add the Boletus. Add broth, one ladleful at a time, stirring until absorbed into the rice mixture. Continue this way, adding broth one ladleful at a time until all the broth has been incorporated into rice. Add Parmesan cheese, and season to taste. Garnish with almonds and parsley.

Matsutake Risotto

Recipe by Ryane Snow.

> *Serves 6 to 8*
>
> 1 6-inch Matsutake or 2 smaller ones, chopped (about 1 to 1½ cups)
>
> ½ medium onion, chopped
>
> 2 tablespoons butter
>
> 1 cup short grain white rice (arborio)
>
> 4 cups chicken broth (low salt or unsalted)
>
> 2 tablespoons minced celery (optional)
>
> 2 tablespoons Parmesan cheese, grated
>
> Miso or soy sauce to taste
>
> 2 tablespoons slivered toasted almonds (optional garnish)
>
> 1 tablespoon minced cilantro (optional, or may use parsley)

Heat the broth to a low simmer. Meanwhile, in a separate 6 to 8-cup saucepan, melt the butter over medium-to-low heat and sauté the onions and mushrooms until tender. Add the rice and sauté, stirring constantly, until rice has begun to toast very slightly. Add the broth, one ladleful at a time, stirring until it is absorbed into the rice mixture. Continue this way, adding broth one ladleful at a time and stirring to incorporate. Add the celery with the last ladleful of broth. When all broth is absorbed into the risotto, stir in the Parmesan cheese and soy sauce or miso to taste. Garnish with almonds and cilantro.

Kasha with Mushrooms

Recipe by Irina Valioulina.

This recipe is good with any mushroom.

Serves 4

1 to 2 cups mushrooms, chopped

1 tablespoon butter or oil

1 cup buckwheat groats

½ teaspoon salt or to taste

Sauté the mushrooms in the butter until they are well cooked. Add the buckwheat, and sauté, stirring constantly, until the buckwheat is toasted. Pour in 2 cups of water and the salt, bring to a boil, cover and turn down to low heat, and simmer a 20 to 30 minutes, until the water is absorbed. Turn the heat down to the lowest setting, or put it in the oven at 250° F, and let the kasha cook slowly for another half hour to an hour, to dry and fluff it, then serve.

Shrimp Russula with Rice

Recipe by Irina Valioulina.

Serves 4

1 cup rice

2 to 3 cups shrimp russula, chopped

2 tablespoon butter or oil

Cook the rice in a small saucepan with 2 cups of water until almost done (time depends on the type of rice).

In a frying pan over medium-high heat, fry the shrimp mushroom in the butter or oil until they are crunchy. Add the rice and cook them together in the frying pan, adding a little more water as necessary, until the rice is completely cooked.

Baked Oyster Mushrooms

This recipe is reprinted from Gathered Mushroom Recipes, *a booklet by Teresa Sholars' fall 1981 mushroom class at the Fort Bragg branch of College of the Redwoods.*

Serves 6 to 8

6 cups oyster mushrooms

¼ cup butter

2 cups bread crumbs

¼ cup Parmesan cheese

2 tablespoons minced parsley

½ teaspoon salt

Pinch of pepper

Preheat the oven to 300° F. Sauté the mushrooms in 1 tablespoon of the butter for 10 minutes.

Melt the remaining butter, and toss it with the crumbs, Parmesan, parsley, salt and pepper, in a bowl.

In an 8-inch-square glass baking dish, layer half the mushrooms, then half the bread, the remaining mushrooms, and top with the remaining bread. Bake for 45 minutes to an hour, or until crumbs are starting to brown.

Clavariadelphus Green Bean Casserole

Recipe by Teddy Winslow.

Serves 6

1 pound green beans

3 onions

10 *Clavariadelphus truncatus* (Flat-Topped Club Coral Mushroom)

½ cup butter

½ cup Parmesan cheese

1 cup bread crumbs

1 cup slivered or sliced almonds

Preheat the oven to 350° F. String the beans and cut them into 2" pieces. Chop the onions. Slice the mushrooms cross-wise, or at a diagonal. Put the onions and mushrooms with the beans into a large bowl. Melt ¼ cup of the butter and pour it over the bean mixture. Add Parmesan and toss. Put the mixture into a suitable casserole dish, cover and bake for 1 hour.

Melt the remaining ¼ cup butter in a skillet. Fry the bread crumbs in it until they begin to brown. Remove from heat and add the almonds. When the casserole is done, sprinkle with the bread and almond topping and serve.

Peas or Green Beans with Milk Caps

This can also be made with blewits for a different color variation, or combine the two mushrooms for green, orange and purple!

Serves 4 to 6

2 cups peas or green beans

½ cup chopped onion

1 cup chopped *Lactarius deliciosus* or *L. sanguifluus*

2 cloves garlic

1 tablespoon butter

Pinch of nutmeg

Sauté the onions and mushrooms in 1 teaspoon of the butter over low heat in a lidded pan, stirring occasionally, until the onions are translucent. Mince the garlic and add it, sautéing a few minutes longer. Meanwhile, steam the peas or beans until just done. Combine the two in a serving bowl, toss in a pinch of nutmeg and the rest of the butter.

Blewits with Peas and Carrots

Serves 4

1 cup chopped blewits

½ cup chopped onion

1 tablespoon butter

2 cups fresh shelled or frozen green peas

½ cup chopped carrot

¼ teaspoon grated lemon or orange rind

Pinch of nutmeg or mace

Sauté the blewits and onion in the butter until the onion is translucent. Meanwhile, steam the carrots until tender. Add the peas and steam 3 to 5 minutes longer. Put into a serving bowl, stir in the mushrooms and onions, the rind and the nutmeg. Serve immediately.

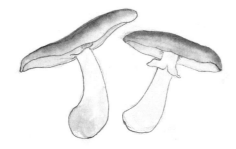

Deer Mushroom With Asparagus

Deer mushrooms can sometimes be found late enough in the spring that asparagus is available—the flavors go well together.

Serves 4 as side dish

2 tablespoons butter or oil

3 cups asparagus, cut in 1-inch pieces

½ onion, diced

2 cups fresh or frozen *Pluteus cervinus*, sliced

½ cup chopped almonds

2 cloves garlic, minced or pressed

Grated rind of a lemon or an orange

¼ teaspoon nutmeg

2 tablespoons soy sauce, or to taste

Melt the butter in a frying pan. Add the asparagus. After it turns bright green, add the onions. When the onions begin to get translucent, add the mushrooms and nuts. When nearly done, add the garlic. When the vegetables are done, stir in the orange rind and nutmeg, season with soy sauce, and serve.

Morel and Bok Choy Stir-Fry

Serves 4

16 morels, fresh or dried

1 small onion

2 tablespoons butter or light-flavored oil

2 thin slices fresh ginger

10 stalks of large bok choy or 2 heads of baby bok choy

4 cloves garlic

1 cup water or chicken or vegetable stock (if morels are fresh)

1 tablespoon miso or soy sauce

1 teaspoon cornstarch

Dash of toasted sesame oil (3 drops)

Cut the morels in half lengthwise and clean out any debris, bugs, or slugs. If the mushrooms are dried, put them in hot water to soak for about ½ hour. Drain and reserve the soaking water.

Chop the onion, put it in a skillet with the butter or oil, and sauté, stirring often. Mince the ginger and add to pan.

Chop the bok choy, separating the stems from the leaves. When the onions begin to get translucent add the bok choy stems and the mushrooms. Mince the garlic and add, along with the bok choy leaves, when the stems begin to tender. Using 1 cup reserved morel soaking liquid, or the stock, make a mixture with the cornstarch and the miso or soy sauce. Mix well until smooth, and add it to the skillet, stirring constantly until sauce thickens slightly and boils. Turn off the heat and stir in the sesame oil. Serve over rice.

Mushroom Rice Stuffing

This is an excellent gluten-free alternative, best with the savory mushrooms, such as sweetbread, man-on-horseback, horn-of-plenty, yellow foot, or boletes.

Makes enough stuffing for a chicken or duck; for a turkey, multiply by 3 or 4

1 cup uncooked rice, brown, white or a blend with wild rice

½ cup chopped onion

½ cup chopped celery

2 cups fresh chopped mushrooms*

2 tablespoons minced parsley or chervil

½ teaspoon sage

½ teaspoon basil

½ teaspoon thyme

1 teaspoon salt

* If any mushrooms are dried, soak them in hot water until soft, reserving the water for the rice.

Put the rice in a saucepan with ¾ cup water (including any mushroom-soaking water), and cook until water is just absorbed; 15 to 20 minutes for white rice, or about 30 minute for brown.

Mix the partially-cooked rice with all other ingredients, and stuff the bird. Cook according to instructions on the package for cooking a stuffed bird of that size. If you are cooking the stuffing separately, put it in a baking dish with ¼ cup water, cover tightly, and bake at 350° F. for ½ hour, in a preheated oven.

Turkey Dressing with Candy Caps

Recipe by Erif Thunen.

This makes enough to stuff the turkey and bake some separately also.
Makes about 10 cups

4 cups bread diced into cubes (½ loaf, not too dark-flavored)

2 cups onions, diced

2 cups apples, diced

½ to 1 cup dried candy cap mushrooms, or 1 to 2 cups fresh

1 cup pecans, chopped coarsely

6 cloves garlic, chopped finely

1 tablespoon fresh sage, chopped finely, or 1 teaspoon dried

¼ cup parsley, chopped finely

1 tablespoon salt

½ teaspoon pepper

1 egg (optional)

Water or milk to moisten

Preheat the oven. In a large bowl toss together the bread, onions, apple, mushrooms, pecans, garlic, sage, parsley, salt and pepper. Stir in the egg, if using. Add water or milk to moisten the dressing, starting with a cup and adding more, ½ cup at a time until it is as moist as you prefer in a dressing.

Stuff it in a bird and bake it, per directions for the bird, or put the stuffing into greased baking pans and bake at 350° F for about 45 minutes or until the onions are soft and the dressing is browning on top.

Fruited Candy Cap Stuffing

This is a sweeter stuffing, bread-based, with fruit. If you are using a packaged stuffing mix, you may use the seasoning packet that comes with it and omit the salt, sage and thyme. For stuffing a chicken, divide recipe by 4, but use one whole egg.

Makes enough to stuff a turkey, and bake some separately.

8 cups stale bread cubes

4 apples, cored and chopped

2 onions, chopped

2 cups chopped celery

2 cups raisins

1 cup whole cranberries

1 cup chopped dates

2 cups chopped fresh candy caps, or ½ cup chopped dried

2 eggs

Milk

2 tablespoons salt or to taste

1 teaspoon sage

1 tablespoon thyme

½ teaspoon nutmeg

Mix the bread, fruits, vegetables and mushrooms together in a large mixing bowl. Stir in the eggs, and enough milk to moisten the bread well. Mix in the seasonings, and stuff the turkey, and bake per stuffed turkey instructions. Put the leftover stuffing in baking dishes, and put them in the oven 45 minutes before the turkey is done. If not baking a turkey, bake the stuffing at 350° F, in a preheated oven, for 30 to 45 minutes, or until browning on top.

Matsutake-Cabbage Stuffing

This recipe is particularly good with duck, as it doesn't absorb fat like a bread stuffing will. To stuff a turkey, multiply recipe by 3 or 4. Recipe inspired by Judy Bonney.

Makes about a quart, for stuffing a chicken or duck

2 cups (packed) chopped Chinese cabbage

1 cup sliced matsutake

1 cup pineapple, fresh or canned

3 green onions, chopped

1 teaspoon soy sauce

¼ teaspoon sesame oil

Pinch of nutmeg

½ cup chopped, toasted cashews (optional)

Mix all ingredients, and stuff into a bird. Bake as instructed for a stuffed bird. If baking separately from the bird, put in a covered glass or ceramic casserole, and bake in a preheated 350° F oven for ½ hour.

Candy Cap Baked Beans

This may be cooked on top of the stove and in the oven, or the whole process may be done in a large crock pot.

Makes about 12 servings

3 cups pinto or other dry beans

1 bay leaf

1 medium onion, chopped

⅓ cup brown sugar

1 teaspoon salt

2 tablespoons tomato paste or ¼ cup ketchup

1 cup fresh minced or ¼ cup dried ground candy caps

2 tablespoons vinegar (halve if using ketchup instead of tomato paste)

½ teaspoon dry mustard or 1 tablespoon prepared mustard

4 cloves garlic, minced

1 cup diced ham, hot dogs, or bacon (optional)

½ cup smoked pig's ear mushrooms (optional, see recipe on page 255)

Soak the beans overnight, in water to cover. Drain.

Cover the beans with water again, an inch or two above the top of the beans. Put the bay leaf in the pot, and cook beans until they are barely done, but still a bit firm. (Stove top, about 2 to 3 hours, in a crock pot on high, 4 to 6 hours). Drain off the excess water, reserving for later if needed. If baking in the oven, preheat it now to 250° F.

Return ½ cup of bean cooking liquid to pot of beans. Add all other ingredients, and place in lidded casserole dish in the oven or leave in the crock pot on the medium setting.

Cook covered, for 2 to 3 hours, stirring occasionally and adding more of the reserved liquid as needed if the beans dry out. Serve when beans are soft and flavors have melded.

Candy Cap Applesauce

Serves 4

3 to 4 apples

6 to 8 candy caps, fresh or dried

½ teaspoon cinnamon (optional)

Core and chop the apples. (Peel first if desired.) Mince the mushrooms. Put in the apples and mushrooms in a small saucepan, and add ¼ cup of water. Cover and bring to a boil. Turn down to low heat and simmer 10 to 15 minutes, until the apples are soft, checking occasionally and adding a little water if necessary to prevent burning. When done, mash apples with a fork and stir in the cinnamon. Serve warm or cold. For a sweeter version, see the recipe on page 221.

Country Fried Russulas

Serve with or without melted cheese on top. May be made with Russula xerampolina, R. brevipes *or the lobster mushroom.*

Serves 4

3 slices of bacon

½ onion, chopped

2 large potatoes or 3 smaller (about 2½ cups quartered and thinly sliced)

3 to 4 *Russula cyanoxantha* (2½ to 3 cups sliced)

½ teaspoon thyme

½ teaspoon paprika

Salt and pepper to taste

½ cup grated jack or cheddar cheese (optional)

Chop the bacon and to fry it in a large skillet. When it's done, pour off and reserve excess grease, and drain the bacon on paper towels. Add the chopped onion to the skillet, along with the sliced mushrooms and potatoes. Cook until the potatoes are soft adding a little bacon grease as necessary. Sprinkle in the thyme, paprika, salt and pepper halfway through the cooking process, and stir occasionally with a sharp spatula to prevent potatoes from sticking. Remove from heat when done, and stir in the bacon. If desired, sprinkle with grated cheese, cover pan, and let stand until the cheese melts. May be served as a side-dish for either breakfast or dinner.

Entrées

Princely Bisteeya

A bisteeya is a festive Moroccan meat pie combining sweet and savory flavors in a phyllo dough crust.

Serves 12 to 15

4 chicken thighs

1½ cups rose petals (packed), or ½ cup rose water

2 teaspoons cinnamon

¼ teaspoon ginger

¼ teaspoon cardamom

¾ teaspoon salt

4 cups *Agaricus augustus*

1 onion

1 T olive oil

2 cloves garlic

1 cup sliced or chopped toasted almonds

2 tablespoons honey

4 eggs

Grated rind and juice of 1 lemon

2 cups spinach

¼ cup fresh basil

1 cup butter

1 package phyllo dough, thawed

Put the chicken in a large saucepan with 2 cups of water. Put ½ cup of the rose petals in the blender with 2 cups water, 1 teaspoon of the cinnamon, the other spices and ¼ teaspoon of the salt. Purée and add to chicken. If you do not have rose petals, add ¼ cup of the rose water to the chicken pot, along with 2 cups of water, 1 teaspoon of the cinnamon and the other spices, and ¼ teaspoon of the salt. Bring the chicken to a boil, lid the pot and turn down to a simmer. Simmer for 1 hour. Cool, reserving both the stock and the chicken.

Chop the mushroom and mince the onion. Sauté in the olive oil until the onions are translucent and the mushrooms are cooked through. Mince the garlic and add it; sauté another few minutes. Set aside to cool. Mix the almonds and the honey, warming the honey if it is too stiff to mix in well. Set aside.

Remove the chicken from the stock, and reheat the stock. Beat the eggs, and add them to the stock, stirring constantly over low heat until it sets. Remove from heat and set aside.

Bone the chicken, chop the meat, and mix in the remaining salt and cinnamon, and the lemon rind and juice. If rose petals are not available, mix the remaining rose water into the chicken. Set aside.

If using rose petals, mince the remaining cup and set aside. Chop the spinach, mince the basil, and combine them. Set aside.

Preheat the oven to 400° F.

Melt the butter. Using a pastry brush and a small amount of the butter, butter the bottom and sides of a 9-by-13-inch baking pan. Cut the phyllo sheets in half cross-wise, so they are approximately 9 by 13 inches. Lay a sheet of phyllo in the bottom of the pan, keeping the remaining sheets under a damp dishtowel or plastic.

Brush butter on the phyllo and top with another sheet. Continue in this way until you have stacked about 10 sheets of phyllo dough with butter brushed between each sheet, and on top. Sprinkle on the spinach, and top with 2 sheets of dough, brushed with butter. Sprinkle on the rose petals, and top with 2 sheets of dough, brushed with butter.

Spread on the egg-thickened stock, and top with 2 sheets of dough, brushed with butter.

Spread on the chicken, and top with 2 sheets of dough, brushed with butter.

Sprinkle on ¾ cup of the nut mixture, and top with 2 sheets of dough, brushed with butter.

Spread on the mushroom-onion mixture, and top with the remaining sheets of phyllo dough, brushing each one and the top with butter. Sprinkle the remaining nuts on top, and bake for 25 to 40 minutes, or until the phyllo dough begins to brown.

Boletus Mock Scallops

Recipe by Nikolai Sprinkling, who says "When I served this to my friends, they thought it was real scallops."

Serves 2 to 4

2 to 4 Nice plump *Boletus edulis* with thick firm stems.

1 egg

1 cup bread crumbs

2 to 3 tablespoons (or more) crumbled seaweed of your choice

1 teaspoon sea salt

2 tablespoons peanut oil or sesame oil or other heat-stable oil

Clean the mushrooms and remove caps, reserving them for another use.

Slice the stems into rounds about ½ to ¾ inch long, like scallops. Brush all surfaces in egg wash. Cover and let sit 5 minutes while you mix up the bread crumbs with the crumbled seaweed and sea salt in a small bowl. Heat the oil in a large frying pan .

Dip the pieces of mushroom into the flour mixture and fry in the hot oil until the breading begins to crisp, turning to cook both sides and keeping the pieces rather separated in the pan. Only fry enough at once that they lie flat on the bottom of the pan. Remove as they are finished and drain on paper or cloth for several minutes.

E. and B.'s Matsutake Chicken

Recipe by Erif Thunen and Bill Oliveau. Recipe may also be used for rabbit, but omit the thickener. Best started the day before and marinated overnight.

Serves 2 to 4

1½ cups matsutake mushrooms

1 to 2 tablespoons minced ginger

1 teaspoon garlic powder

¼ teaspoon ground black pepper or pepper blend

¼ cup shoyu soy sauce

⅓ cup sherry

1 star anise

1 or 2 green onions

4 chicken thighs, skinned, boned and chopped into bite-sized pieces

oil for frying

½ cup chicken stock

2 teaspoons kudzu or arrowroot or 1 teaspoon cornstarch

2 tablespoons oyster sauce

2 to 3 green onions, sliced for garnish

1 tablespoon toasted sesame seeds

Slice the mushrooms razor-thin; slice the stems on the diagonal. In a large bowl, mix together the ginger, garlic, pepper, soy sauce and sherry. Pound the star anise and add. Mince the 1 or 2 green onions and add. (Or these ingredients could be run through a food processor.) Stir in the mushrooms and chicken. Marinate at least one hour and preferably overnight.

Remove the chicken from the marinade (reserving the marinade) and brown the chicken in oil in a frying pan. Add the marinade with the mushrooms, cover and simmer 40 minutes or until chicken is tender, turning pieces occasionally.

Meanwhile, mix together the chicken broth, thickener and oyster sauce. When chicken is done, stir in this glaze, stirring until it thickens. Remove from heat. Serve, garnishing with sliced green onions and sesame seeds.

Candy Cap or Matsutake Teriyaki Chicken

This recipe is best if allowed to marinate 3 days. You may use a whole chicken and cut it into pieces, or buy an equivalent amount of legs, wings, thighs or breasts, depending on your preference.

Serves 6 to 8

3 to 4 pounds of chicken

1 recipe teriyaki marinade (see recipes on pages 68 and 69)

If you have a whole chicken that has not been disjointed, then cut it into pieces. If you have chicken breasts, you may bone them if you like. Put the chicken pieces in a bowl, and pour the marinade over them. Put plastic or a lid over the top, and marinate in the refrigerator for at least 4 hours, and over-night to 3 days is better, turning pieces over halfway through.

After marinating, preheat the oven to 350° F. Put the chicken and its marinade in a glass baking pan and bake for 45 minutes to an hour, until the meat is done.

If you wish, you may skim the fat (and discard it) from the juice and thicken the pan juice with cornstarch or flour and serve it as sauce.

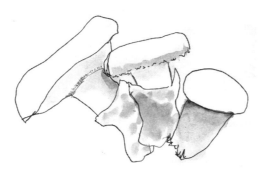

Morels with Asparagus and Scallops

Serves 2

8 morels, fresh or dried

½ small onion, chopped

2 teaspoons butter

2 cups asparagus, cut into 1-inch lengths

½ pound scallops

2 cloves garlic, minced

¼ cup slivered red bell pepper

Salt to taste

Cut the morels in half lengthwise and clean out any debris from inside. If they are dried, cover with hot water and soak half an hour.

Sauté the onion and mushrooms in the butter over medium heat. When the onions begin to soften, add the asparagus. If using large sea scallops add them after 5 minutes of sautéing. If using smaller, bay scallops, wait 10 minutes and add them to the pan mixture. Add the red pepper and minced garlic and sauté until the scallops are just done. Don't overcook the scallops or they will become tough.

Add salt to taste and serve with rice.

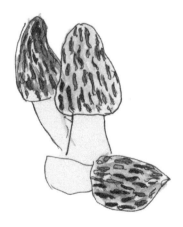

Matsutake Surprise

This recipe is reprinted from Gathered Mushroom Recipes, *a booklet by Teresa Sholars' fall 1981 mushroom class at the Fort Bragg branch of College of the Redwoods.*

Serves 4

8 green onions

4 thin slices ginger root

4 (¼ to ⅓ pound each) fillets rock fish or ling cod

2 cups julienned matsutakes

16 to 20 snow pea or snap pea pods

2 cups broccoli florets

¼ cup sake or white wine

Salt and pepper, if desired

Soy sauce

4 wedges lemon

Preheat the oven to 400° F. Lay out 4 squares of heavy-duty aluminum foil, big enough to completely wrap each fillet with vegetables. Trim the roots from the green onions, split lengthwise, and lay 4 pieces on each square of foil. Put a slice of ginger on top, and then a fillet of fish, and ½ cup of matsutake. Lay 4 or 5 pea pods on the mushroom, then the broccoli. Sprinkle each serving with a tablespoon of sake or wine, and salt and pepper, if desired. Fold the foil over the top, and fold the edges together, making sealed packets.

Place the packets in a large baking pan, in case any juice escapes, and bake for 20 minutes, or until the fish flakes and the vegetables are steamed. Serve with soy sauce and lemon wedges.

Medieval Pot Roast

The Agaricus augustus *are up and my roses are blooming! What a combo! Roses were often used in cooking meat in the middle ages, and still are in some parts of the middle east. The best roses for cooking are the old, fragrant varieties, moss roses, gallicas, centifolias, damasks, etc. The deep pink to purple varieties give a nice color, as well as flavor. I used my purple moss rose, William Lobb.*

Serves 6 to 8

6 medium to large fragrant roses

1½ to 2 pound pot roast: chuck or round roast

1 tablespoon berry jam or preserves

1 tablespoon cider or red wine vinegar

2 nice big prince mushrooms

1 onion

1 tablespoon butter

3 carrots

1 beet (optional)

¼ cup red wine

1 to 2 teaspoons salt, or to taste

Puree the roses in a blender with 2 to 3 cups water. Put the roast into a pot or crock pot, along with the rose puree and another quart of water, the jam, and the vinegar. Simmer on top of the stove for about 4 hours, or in the crock pot for about 6 hours, or until the meat is tender, replacing water as it boils down.

Slice the princes, and chop the onion. Melt the butter in a frying pan and saute the mushroom and onion until the mushroom is cooked and the onions translucent. Add them to the pot.

Slice the carrots, and julienne the beets. Chop the beet tops and set aside. Add the carrots and beets to the pot, and simmer 15 minutes.

Add the beet tops, the wine and the salt. Simmer 3 minutes. Pull the roast apart with two forks into chunks. Serve in bowls with broth.

Bread may be served to sop up the broth, if desired.

Admirable Mirabilis Fish

Serves 4

1 large *Boletus mirabilis*

1 pound rock fish (snapper) or ling cod fillets

1 tablespoon plus 1 teaspoon butter

⅔ cup water

1 teaspoon dill

2 cloves garlic

1 tablespoon cornstarch

¼ teaspoon salt

Rind and juice of 1 lime and ½ lemon

½ lemon, sliced thinly, for garnish

Sauté the *Boletus mirabilis* in 1 tablespoon butter in a large heavy frying pan. Cook on medium heat stirring occasionally for about 15 minutes.

Meanwhile, make the sauce. In a small saucepan sauté the garlic in the remaining teaspoon of butter until fragrant. Add water, dill, salt, lemon rind and lime rind.

In a small cup, mix the lemon and lime juice with the cornstarch. When sauce boils add the lemon/cornstarch mixture and stir until thickened. Keep the sauce warm on low heat.

Spread the cooked *Boletus* to cover entire pan and lay the fillets of fish atop the mushrooms in a single layer, arranging them to fit by cutting if necessary. Cover and poach the fish until the edges are opaque. Flip the fish and cover, cooking a few more minutes until fish flakes when poked with a fork, and is done. Serve the fish topped with the mushroom, with the warm sauce and a lemon garnish.

Mushroom and Cashew Stroganoff

Recipe from Cynthia Frank.

Serves 4 to 6

1 cup raw cashews (whole or pieces)

1 to 2 tablespoons tamari or mushroom soy sauce

⅓ cup butter

1½ cups thinly sliced yellow onion (sliced lengthwise)

1 clove crushed garlic

2 pounds mixed fresh mushrooms, sliced

2 tablespoons tomato paste

2 tablespoons Sherry or Madeira wine

1½ cups sour cream

Salt and freshly ground pepper, to taste

4 tablespoons minced fresh flat-leaf parsley

Brown rice or buttered, wide noodles.

Preheat oven to 350° F.

Melt the butter in a large frying pan. Add the onions and sauté on low heat until caramelized. Add the crushed garlic and stir thoroughly.

While the onions are caramelizing, spread cashews in a single layer on a cookie sheet and roast in oven for 6 minutes.

Sprinkle with tamari, stir, and put back in oven for another 5 minutes.

Turn off the oven, stir the cashews again, and leave in oven for an additional 5 minutes.

Remove from oven and let cool.

Add the mushrooms to the onions and garlic and cook, stirring, until they have softened and released their juices. Stir in the tomato paste and wine. Cook for another 2 to 3 minutes.

Remove from heat; stir in the sour cream and 2 tablespoons parsley. Season with salt and pepper.

Serve over brown rice or buttered noodles. Sprinkle with the tamari-roasted cashews and reminder of the chopped parsley.

Boletus with Liver

Serves 4

1 tablespoon butter

1 medium sized *Boletus edulis* or *Leccinum manzanitae* (not more than half open)

1 onion, sliced

1 pound liver sliced (or whole if chicken liver is used)

1 bell pepper, chopped

Slice the mushrooms. (If using *Leccinum*, par-boil it before sautéing.)

Sauté the mushrooms and onions in the butter until nearly done. Turn down heat and add the bell pepper and liver, sautéing the liver gently on both sides until just done. Remove from fire while moist and tender, and serve.

Stuffed Subrutilescens

Recipe by Lucien Long of Elk. He originally invented it for Portabellas. This hearty dish may be served as either a vegetarian entrée or a side dish.

Serves 4

1 red onion, sliced

1 tablespoon olive oil

4 large, open *Agaricus subrutilescens* caps

½ cup pesto (or see recipe for chanterelle pesto on page 66)

¼ cup crumbled feta cheese

¼ cup crumbled queso fresco

Preheat the oven to 350° F. Sauté the red onion in the oil until it caramelizes. Lay the mushroom caps out on a cookie sheet. Divide the onions between the caps. Spoon 2 tablespoons of pesto on top of the onions for each serving, then top with 1 tablespoon of each cheese per mushroom cap. Bake about 20 to 30 minutes. Serve.

Amanita Calyptrata Suprème

Recipe by Erif Thunen.

Serves 2

1 large, open *Amanita calyptrata (A. calyptroderma)*

1 teaspoon butter

1 teaspoon olive oil

2 small or 1 large shallot, chopped

1 tablespoon minced parsley

2 cloves garlic, minced

½ teaspoon chicken masala powder or curry powder

1 tablespoon half-and-half

¼ cup bread crumbs (optional)

1 tablespoon cream or 1 teaspoon melted butter (optional)

Cut the *Amanita* stalk from the cap. Melt ½ teaspoon of the butter in a frying pan and add ½ teaspoon of the olive oil. Sauté the mushroom cap on the top side only (gills up) until it softens. Set aside. Preheat the oven to 350° F.

Slice and dice the mushroom stalk, and add it to the frying pan along with the remaining ½ teaspoon of butter and olive oil, and begin to sauté. Add the shallots and sauté until they begin to soften. Add the garlic, parsley, masala or curry powder and the half-and-half. Sauté until it smells exquisite.

Place the mushroom cap onto a baking sheet, gill side up, and spoon the filling onto it. For the optional bread topping, combine the bread crumbs with the cream or melted butter and sprinkle over the filling. Bake for ½ hour or if using the bread topping, until it is golden brown. Serve.

Mushrooms Charlie

Recipe from Cynthia Frank.
A nice side for steak, roast pork, roast tofu, burgers of any kind.

Serves 6

1 yellow onion, cut in half and sliced

½ cup butter

1 pound cleaned, fresh mushrooms (choose your favorite, meaty varieties), cut in half.

1 red pepper, cut in 1-inch dice

1 green pepper, cut in 1-inch dice

2 tablespoons country-style Dijon mustard

2 tablespoons Worcestershire sauce

2 tablespoons molasses

¾ cup full-bodied red wine

½ teaspoon thyme

salt

fresh-cracked pepper

Melt the butter in a large saucepan and sauté the onions slowly until they start to turn golden.

While the onions are caramelizing, whisk together the mustard, Worcestershire sauce, molasses, red wine, and thyme in a small bowl. Set aside so the flavors can marry.

Add the mushrooms and peppers to the caramelizing onions and cook slowly for another 10 minutes. Stir often, to make sure the bottom doesn't scorch.

Add the sauce mixture and stir thoroughly. Simmer the mixture over medium heat for about 45 minutes or until the sauce is much reduced and thickened.

Season to taste with salt and pepper.

Lamb and Wine-Agaric Stuffed Bread

Recipe by Bill Oliveau. Bill prefers to use wine agarics in this recipe, but Agaricus campestris, *or* A. fuscofibrillosus, *or even portabellos will make an excellent dish.*

Serves 6

1 red onion, diced

1 tablespoon olive oil

5 cloves garlic

1 teaspoon ground cumin

1 teaspoon paprika

1½ pounds lamb stew meat, cut into ¾ inch dice

1 teaspoon salt

¼ teaspoon pepper

2 bay leaves

1 bottle of dark beer

1 bouillon cube

1 large or 2 medium-sized leeks

4 to 6 robust wine agarics, about 3 cups, diced

1 round loaf of bread, Ciabatta or sourdough

½ pound Jarlsburg or Swiss cheese, grated

Sauté the onion in a large frying pan in the olive oil until it is translucent. Add the garlic, cumin and paprika, and sauté until fragrant. Add the lamb and the salt and pepper, and sauté, stirring, until the lamb is browned. Pour the beer into the pan until the lamb is just covered. Add the bay leaves and bouillon. Bring to a boil, turn down, cover, and simmer for 1 to 1½ hours or until lamb is tender. Uncover and simmer until the liquid is reduced to a sauce. Slice the leeks into ½ inch rounds, discarding the tough ends of the leaves. Add the leeks and mushrooms to the pan. Remove from heat, cover and let the leeks and mushrooms steam over the meat.

Preheat the oven to 350° F. Cut a lid off the top of the loaf of bread. Hollow out the loaf and the lid, saving the bread for another purpose if desired. Stir the leeks and mushrooms into the lamb. Layer the lamb and mushroom filling into the bread, alternating with layers of cheese. Start with the lamb and end with the cheese, creating 3 or 4 layers.

For a crisp crust on the bread, place on a cookie sheet in the oven. Bake 30 to 45 minutes, and serve. For a soft crust, wrap the loaf in foil and pour ¼ cup beer into the foil before sealing it together at the top. Bake for 1 hour, and serve.

"Beefsteak" Stroganoff

Serves 6 to 8

2 cups chopped beefsteak mushroom

1 onion, chopped

1 pound thinly sliced beef sirloin

1 tablespoon olive oil

4 cloves garlic, chopped

1 cup or more chicken or beef stock

1 (12 to 16-ounce) package egg noodles (or double the recipe on page 90)

1 pint sour cream

1 bay leaf

Salt and pepper to taste

Parmesan cheese

Sauté the mushroom, onion, and beef in the olive oil over medium-high heat until the beef has browned on all sides. Add the bay leaf and garlic, sauté a few minutes, then add broth, turn down the heat and simmer covered for ½ hour, reducing the liquid but adding a little more broth only if necessary to prevent burning.

Meanwhile, boil the noodles, according to the directions on the package. Add the sour cream to the meat mixture and heat slowly to a simmer. Drain the noodles and gently stir them into the cooked meat mixture. Add salt and pepper to taste and serve with Parmesan cheese.

Agaricus Augustus Stroganoff

Recipe by Bill Oliveau.

Put the tri-tip in the freezer about 1 to 2 hours before preparation, to partially freeze it so that it may be sliced more thinly.

Serves 6

1 pound tri-tip

2 to 3 large *Agaricus augustus*

3 tablespoons butter

1 tablespoon olive oil

5 cloves garlic

1 onion

1 to 2 shallots

1 10-ounce package egg noodles (or see recipe on page 90)

½ teaspoon garlic powder

2 tablespoons minced parsley

½ cup dry white wine

1 cup sour cream

Pinch of nutmeg

Salt and pepper to taste

Slice the mushrooms and sauté them in one tablespoon of the butter plus the olive oil until soft and juicy. Remove them from the pan. Slice the onion, shallot and garlic and sauté them together until the onion is translucent.

Meanwhile, boil the noodles according to the instructions on the package. Drain and stir in the remaining 2 tablespoons butter, garlic powder and parsley. Cover tightly and put in the oven at the lowest setting to keep warm.

Retrieve the meat from the freezer, and with a sharp knife, slice it as thinly as possible. Add the meat and mushrooms to the onions. Add the wine and bring to a simmer. Simmer until the wine is reduced down to a few tablespoons. Add the sour cream, nutmeg, salt and pepper. Heat until hot and serve over the noodles.

Sparassis Lasagna

Recipe from Teresa Sholars.

Serves 12 to 15

1 large *Sparassis crispa*

2 bottles spaghetti sauce

1 quart ricotta cheese

½ pound mozzarella, grated

1 cup grated Parmesan cheese

6 cloves garlic, minced, and fresh minced herbs (optional)

2 pounds sausage or hamburger, or a blend of the two (optional)

Preheat the oven to 350° F. Clean the mushroom and trim off the tough area around the stem. (Discard this or use it in soup stock.) Cut the mushroom into noodle-like sections. If it is young and tender, it may be used as is; if it seems tough, parboil it for about 10 to 15 minutes or until it is tender. Stir-fry the sausage or burger until the grease has come out, and drain.

Using a 9 by 13-inch glass baking pan, layer the sauce, mushroom, ricotta cheese, meat, garlic and herbs in the pan, with a little sauce between each layer. Top with Parmesan and mozzarella cheeses. Bake about 45 minutes or until sauce bubbles and cheese is melted.

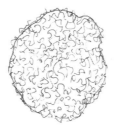

Sparassis Radicata Supreme

This recipe is reprinted from Gathered Mushroom Recipes, *a booklet by Teresa Sholars' fall 1981 mushroom class at the Fort Bragg branch of College of the Redwoods.*

Serves 6 to 8

2 cups *Sparassis radicata*

½ onion chopped

2 tablespoons oil or butter

1 pound asparagus

2 cups bread crumbs

¼ cup melted butter

1 cup half and half

Salt and pepper

Paprika

Put the onion in a skillet with the 2 tablespoons butter or oil and sauté until it is golden.

Meanwhile, trim and clean the mushroom. If it seems old or tough, par-boil it in a quart of water with a tablespoon salt for 10 minutes. Otherwise, cut it into pieces, and add it to the skillet with the onion, after the onion becomes translucent. Preheat the oven to 375° F.

Cut up the asparagus and steam it lightly, until bright green and just tender.

In a bowl, mix the crumbs with the ¼ cup melted butter and the half and half. Spread half the crumbs in the bottom of a buttered 6-cup casserole. Spread the mushroom and onion mixture over the crumbs, then the asparagus. Sprinkle with salt and pepper, and top with the remaining crumbs. Sprinkle paprika over the top and bake for 25 minutes.

Mushroom Ratatouille

This recipe is reprinted from Gathered Mushroom Recipes, *a booklet by Teresa Sholars' fall 1981 mushroom class at the Fort Bragg branch of College of the Redwoods.*

Serves 8 to 12

4 cups cauliflower mushroom

1 medium eggplant, or 1 large zucchini, or 3 cups puffball, diced

3 tablespoons olive oil

1 clove garlic

1½ cups fresh tomatoes or 1 (15-ounce) can

2 bell peppers, sliced

¼ teaspoon marjoram

Salt and pepper to taste

If using eggplant, sprinkle it liberally with salt and allow to sit for 15 minutes. Rinse.

Meanwhile, clean and cut the cauliflower mushroom into bite-sized pieces, discarding any tough parts. If the mushroom seems old or tough, par-boil it in 2 quarts of water with 2 tablespoons salt for 10 minutes.

Sauté the cauliflower mushroom, and eggplant, puffball or zucchini, and garlic in a large frying pan, in the olive oil, over medium heat, until the eggplant or zucchini are almost done. Add the tomatoes, bell pepper and marjoram. Cook a few minutes longer.

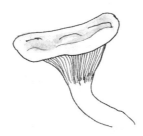

Boletus Edulis Lasagna

Serves 12 to 15

1 large eggplant (optional)

salt

olive oil

1 box lasagna noodles

2 pounds *Boletus edulis* buttons or 1 quart dried boletes

1 pound sausage (optional)

2 pounds spinach (optional)

About 1 quart marinara sauce (if using spinach, you could use Alfredo sauce)

1 pint ricotta cheese

6 cloves garlic, minced

1 (4-inch) sprig rosemary, or 2 teaspoons dry

2 (4-inch) sprigs marjoram or oregano, or 1 tablespoon dry

3 (3-inch) sprigs thyme, or 2 teaspoons dry

½ pound mozzarella cheese, grated

¼ pound Parmesan cheese, grated

If using eggplant, slice, sprinkle both sides of each slice with salt, and let stand for 15 minutes to ½ hour.

Bring at least a gallon of water to a boil in a large pot. Add 4 tablespoons salt and 1 tablespoon oil. Add the lasagna noodles one at a time to the pot. Stir frequently until the noodles soften. Boil for 10 to 15 minutes or per the instructions on the box. They should be soft but not mushy. Pour off half the water, and replace with cold water to stop the cooking and cool the pasta.

If using fresh boletes, slice the mushrooms and sauté lightly in olive oil; set aside. If using dried, cut them into bite-sized pieces and soak them in hot water until they are soft; drain and set aside.

Rinse eggplant slices and sauté them in olive oil until they are done; set aside. Fry the sausage and drain off the fat; set aside. Steam the spinach; set aside. Mince the herbs, discarding the stems. Mix the herbs and garlic in to the ricotta cheese. Preheat the oven to 350° F.

Using a 9 by 13-inch glass baking pan, put a thin layer of sauce on the bottom, then a single layer of noodles. Spread the sauce sparingly. Layer eggplant, sausage, and/or spinach, mushroom, ricotta, and noodles with the sauce, using 3 layers of noodles, top, middle, and bottom. Top with sauce, then grated mozzarella and Parmesan cheese. Bake about 45 minutes or until the sauce bubbles and the cheese is melted.

Quick Lasagna Method

Do not cook the noodles or the spinach. Layer as above, making sure there is a layer of pasta sauce over or under each layer of pasta. The top layer of pasta must be covered with sauce, then the cheese. Pour ½ cup of water into the lasagna, cover tightly with foil. Bake for 45 minutes, uncover and bake an additional 10 minutes. Serve.

Fistulina Lamb Curry

Serves 4

1 tablespoon coconut oil

1 carrot sliced

½ cup chopped celery

½ onion, chopped

1 bell pepper, chopped

1 pound ground lamb

3 cups diced *Fistulina hepatica*

1 apple, cored and chopped

4 cloves garlic, chopped

2 tablespoons curry powder

1 teaspoon cinnamon

¼ cup raisins or chopped prunes

1 cup water or meat or vegetable stock

½ cup coconut milk

1 bay leaf

3 whole cloves

In large stainless steel frying pan, melt the coconut oil, then sauté the carrot, celery, and onion until the onion becomes translucent. Add the bell pepper, lamb, *Fistulina hepatica*, and apple and sauté until the apple is tender. Add the garlic, curry powder, and cinnamon, and sauté one minute more. Add the raisins, water or stock, coconut milk, bay leaf and cloves and simmer for 20 minutes, until liquid has reduced and thickened slightly. Serve over rice.

Mushroom Pizza with Red Sauce

Makes one 12-inch pizza.

Dough for one pizza (see recipe on page 77)

2 cups tomato sauce

1 onion, sliced

4 cups sliced mushrooms

1 tablespoon olive oil

4 ounces pastrami or pepperoni (optional)

6 cloves garlic

2 cups grated mozzarella or provolone cheese

¼ cup grated Parmesan cheese

1 to 2 tablespoons fresh herbs, finely chopped (optional)

Preheat the oven to 425° F. If you are using a pizza stone, preheat it in the oven.

Throw, stretch or roll out the dough to a 12-inch round, or to fit your pan. Place the dough on the pan. (If using a pizza stone, roll the dough out on a floured board, and transfer it later.) Spread the dough with the tomato sauce, and arrange the onions, mushrooms, and salami slices on top. Mince the garlic and sprinkle it evenly over the pizza. Sprinkle on the cheeses, and the fresh herbs, if available. If using a pizza stone, slide the pizza off the board onto the hot stone. Otherwise, put the pan or baking sheet into the oven. Bake 12 to 20 minutes, rotating every 5 minutes, until the crust is browning, the cheese melted and the mushrooms are cooked.

Teriyaki Matsutake Pizza

Makes one 12-inch pizza

Dough for one pizza (see recipe on page 77)

2 cups matsutake teriyaki sauce (see recipe on page 68), or regular teriyaki sauce

1 onion, sliced

4 cups sliced matsutakes

1 can pineapple rings or chunks

½ cup grated mozzarella cheese (optional)

¼ cup grated Parmesan cheese

Preheat the oven to 450° F. If you are using a pizza stone, preheat it in the oven.

Stretch the dough to a 12-inch round, or to fit your pan. Place the dough on the pan. (If using a pizza stone, roll the dough out on a floured board, and transfer later.) Spread the dough with the teriyaki sauce. Arrange the onion and mushrooms slices on the dough. Arrange the pineapple on top. Sprinkle on the cheeses. If using a pizza stone, slide the pizza off the board onto the preheated stone. Otherwise, put the pan or baking sheet into the oven. Bake 12 to 20 minutes, turning every 5 minutes, until the crust is browning, the mushrooms cooked and the cheese melted.

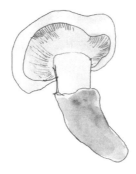

Mushroom Pizza with White Sauce

Use a store bought Alfredo sauce or make your own. This is excellent using the Agaricus augustus Alfredo sauce recipe with A. augustus *mushrooms!*

Makes one 12-inch pizza

Dough for one pizza (see recipe on page 77)

2 cups Alfredo sauce (see recipe on page 61)

1 onion, sliced

4 cups sliced mushrooms

6 cloves garlic

1 cup chopped chicken or ham (optional)

2 cups grated mozzarella or provolone cheese

¼ cup grated Parmesan cheese

1 to 2 tablespoons fresh herbs, finely chopped (optional)

Preheat the oven to 425° F. If you are using a pizza stone, preheat it in the oven.

Stretch the dough to a 12-inch round, or to fit your pan. Place the dough on the pan. (If using a pizza stone, roll the dough out on a floured board, and transfer later.) Spread the dough with the Alfredo sauce, and arrange the onions, mushrooms and meat on the dough. Mince the garlic and sprinkle it evenly over the pizza. Sprinkle on the cheeses, and the fresh herbs, if available. If using a pizza stone, slide the pizza off the board onto the hot stone. Otherwise, put the pan or baking sheet into the oven. Bake 12 to 20 minutes, rotating every 5 minutes, until the crust is browning, the cheese melted, and the mushrooms and onions are cooked.

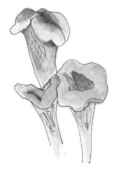

Mushroom Meat Loaf

This may be made with any savory edible mushroom, with the results differing in flavor. All the ingredients may be quickly minced in a food processor.

Serves 8

2 to 3 cups chopped or minced mushrooms

1 tablespoon butter or oil

1½ pounds ground beef

¼ cup minced onion

½ bell pepper, minced

¼ cup minced celery or 2 tablespoons minced parsley

1 egg

½ to 1 cup bread crumbs

1 teaspoon salt

¼ teaspoon ground black pepper

¼ cup ketchup or tomato sauce

Grease a loaf pan and preheat the oven to 350° F. Sauté the mushrooms in the oil until they release their water and the water has evaporated, Mix together the ground beef, mushrooms, onion, bell pepper, celery or parsley, egg, bread crumbs, and salt and pepper. Pack the mixture into a greased loaf pan and spread the top with ketchup or tomato sauce. Bake for 1 hour at 350° F. Remove from oven and allow to rest 10 minutes, slice and serve.

Chanterelle Chicken Pot Pie

Serves 8, makes one 9-inch deep dish pie.

Pie crust for double-crust pie (see recipe on page 253)

2 cups torn chanterelles

2 cups diced cooked chicken

½ cup chopped carrot

1 cup chopped onion

½ cup chopped celery

1 cup diced potatoes

1 teaspoon thyme, fresh if possible

½ teaspoon rosemary, fresh if possible

1 teaspoon salt

1 tablespoon butter

¼ cup flour

Preheat the oven to 350° F. Sauté the chanterelles in butter 5 to 10 minutes, until they exude their liquid, adding a little water if necessary so that there is a half cup of liquid in the pan with the mushrooms. Set aside. Steam the other vegetables for 5 minutes, until barely tender.

In a large bowl, combine the mushrooms with their liquid, vegetables, and chicken, adding the herbs, salt, and flour. Mix well.

Roll out one half of the pie crust and line a 9-inch deep dish pie pan. Fill with the mushroom mixture. Roll out remaining pie crust, fold it in quarters, and unfold on top of the pie. Seal by pinching the edges all around. Bake for one hour, and serve with a big green salad.

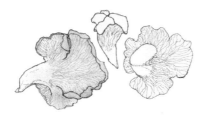

Hedgehog Quiche Lorraine

For a vegetarian version, you could substitute "chanterelle bacon" (see recipe on page 127) for the bacon.

Makes one 9-inch pie, serves 6 to 8

1 unbaked 9-inch pie shell (see recipe on page 253)

6 slices thick-cut bacon, chopped

1 onion, chopped

2 cups chopped hedgehogs

½ cup grated Jarlsberg cheese

3 eggs

1½ cups milk or half-and-half

1 teaspoon thyme

½ teaspoon salt

2 tablespoons grated Parmesan cheese

Preheat the oven to 325° F. Fry the bacon in a frying pan until it is crisp. Drain it on paper towels. Pour most of the grease out of the pan, and sauté the onion and mushrooms in the remainder.

Sprinkle the bacon, onion and mushrooms in the pie shell (in the pie pan). Sprinkle on the Jarlsberg cheese. Whisk together the eggs, milk, thyme, salt and Parmesan, pour into the pie shell, and bake for 40 minutes or until set in the center.

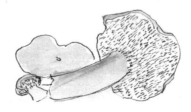

Black Chanterelle and Spinach Quiche

Makes one 9-inch pie, serves 6 to 8

¼ onion, chopped

1 teaspoon butter

2 cups chopped black chanterelles

¼ cup chopped red bell pepper

2 cloves garlic, minced

2 cups chopped fresh spinach or nettles (or frozen)

3 eggs

1 cup milk or half and half

1 cup grated jack cheese

¼ cup grated Parmesan cheese

1 unbaked 9-inch pie shell (see recipe on page 253)

Preheat the oven to 325° F. Sauté the onion in the butter. When translucent, add the mushrooms, garlic, and bell pepper. Sauté about 3 minutes; add the spinach or nettles and continue to sauté until greens are wilted. Remove from heat.

In a mixing bowl, beat the eggs with a fork. Beat in the milk. Stir in the sautéed mushroom and vegetable mixture, and the cheeses. Pour the filling into the pie shell and bake for about 45 minutes to one hour or until set in the center.

Smoky Mushroom Tacos

This is a meat-based taco, that uses smoked pig's ears for flavor.

Makes about 6 tacos

2 cups leftover roast meat—beef, lamb, goat, chicken, turkey, etc.

1 smoked pig's ear mushroom (see recipe on page 255)

1 teaspoon oil or fat

¼ cup broth or pan drippings

½ teaspoon chili powder

⅛ teaspoon cumin

tortillas and other taco fixings of your preference

Mince and sauté the mushroom in the oil or fat, with the chopped leftover meat and spices. Cook for about 5 minutes. Add the broth and simmer just until liquid has fully evaporated. Serve with warm tortillas, cheese, lettuce, cilantro, salsa or whatever you like on your tacos.

Chanterelle Enchiladas

If desired, cooked chicken, pork, or beef may be rolled into the enchiladas also.

Serves 4

4 cups chopped chanterelles

1 teaspoon butter

6 cloves garlic, minced

1 (28-ounce) can enchilada sauce (or see recipe page 67)

8 corn tortillas

½ cup sour cream

sliced black olives

1 cup grated jack or cheddar cheese or queso fresco

Sauté chanterelles in butter until any water has cooked out of them and has mostly evaporated. Add garlic and sauté until fragrant. Set aside while you prepare the enchilada sauce. Preheat the oven to 350° F.

Heat the tortillas either over the flame of a gas stove or in a frying pan on medium-high heat, turning them until they become flexible. Or you may wrap them in a towel and steam them for 1 minute. Then let them rest over the hot water for 10 to 15 minutes.

Spread a spoonful of enchilada sauce over half of the first tortilla, put about ¼ cup chanterelles on it, roll it up and place in a glass baking dish. Repeat with the rest of the tortillas. Pour the remaining sauce over the enchiladas in the pan and top with the shredded cheese. Bake for 20 minutes. Garnish each serving with sour cream and olives.

Stuffed Bell Peppers

This recipe gives 4 stuffed pepper halves. If you wish whole stuffed peppers, the same amount of filling will stuff 3 whole peppers.

Serves 4

¼ cup ground pork sausage or ground lamb

¼ cup chopped onion

1½ cup chopped mushrooms

1 teaspoon olive oil

1 teaspoon curry powder

½ teaspoon cumin

½ teaspoon basil

½ teaspoon salt

1 cup cooked rice or other grain

1 tablespoon tomato paste or ketchup

½ cup grated Havarti, cheddar or provolone cheese

2 bell peppers

Sauté the meat, onion and mushrooms in the oil until the onions are translucent. Add the seasonings, stir a few times, and turn off the heat. Mix in the rice, tomato paste and ¼ cup of the cheese.

Preheat the oven to 350° F. Cut the bell peppers in half, longitudinally through the stem. Leave the stem intact if possible, but scoop out the seeds. Pack ¼ of the mixture into each bell pepper, top with a tablespoon of grated cheese. Put the peppers in a baking dish, and bake for 20 to 25 minutes, until the peppers are tender.

Mild Black Trumpet Curry

Feel free to add any sliced fresh or leftover chicken or other meat to this dish. Just stir into the frying pan with the vegetables and cook all together.

Serves 2

3 to 4 (¼-inch-thick) slices of eggplant

Salt

2 tablespoons coconut oil

½ cup chopped onion

½ cup chopped celery

2 teaspoons curry powder (Indian)

2 cup black trumpet mushrooms

1 cup frozen green peas (or fresh if available)

2 cloves garlic

¼ cup coconut milk

2 tablespoons chopped cilantro for garnish

Salt the eggplant slices on both sides, and let sit for ½ hour. Rinse and dice.

Melt the coconut oil in a frying pan and sauté the eggplant, onions, celery, and curry powder until the onion is translucent. Add the mushrooms, peas, and garlic. Sauté 5 minutes longer. Mix in the coconut milk and salt to taste. bring to a simmer, allow to cook for 3 to 4 minutes. Remove from heat, serve over rice, with a cilantro garnish.

Cabbage Rolls

This is excellent with chanterelles, boletes, black trumpets, yellow feet, spy mushrooms, or most other mushrooms. If using dried mushrooms, use ½ cup, and they may be put in dry; they will rehydrate during the cooking.

Serves 6 to 8

12 to 16 large cabbage leaves, whole

2 cups chopped mushrooms

½ onion, chopped

½ pound bulk Italian sausage (optional)

1 tablespoon olive oil

2 cups cooked rice

1 (14-ounce) can of tomatoes

1 egg

3 cloves garlic, chopped

½ teaspoon salt

¼ teaspoon black pepper

1 teaspoon basil

½ teaspoon oregano

½ teaspoon celery seed

1 (8-ounce) can tomato sauce

Pinch of cayenne

1 cup grated cheese (cheddar, provolone, etc.)

Steam the cabbage leaves for 5 to 10 minutes to soften them. Set aside to cool. Drain the canned tomatoes, reserving the juice. Sauté the mushroom and onion in the olive oil until the mushrooms have exuded their water and it has evaporated. Preheat oven to 350° F.

In a bowl, combine the rice, mushroom, onion, tomatoes, egg, garlic, salt and herbs. Lay a cabbage leaf on a plate or clean cutting board, the stem facing away from you. Put about a half-cup of filling on the end of the cabbage leaf that's towards you; fold in the sides, and roll the filling up in the cabbage leaf. Lay it, open side down, in a glass baking pan. Repeat until all the rolls are made.

Mix the juice drained from the canned tomatoes with the tomato sauce. Add a pinch of cayenne, to taste. Pour this sauce over the cabbage rolls. Bake for ½ hour. Sprinkle with cheese, and return to the oven for 5 minutes, until the cheese is melted.

Turkish Style Cocorra Kebabs

Begin this recipe the day before, allowing the mushrooms to marinate overnight. These kebabs may be made with grisettes, oyster mushrooms or pig's ears, also.

Serves 4

½ teaspoon cumin seed

½ teaspoon coriander seed

½ teaspoon paprika

⅛ teaspoon red pepper flakes

½ teaspoon salt

2 bay leaves

2 cloves of garlic, minced

Grated rind and juice of one lemon

½ cup olive oil

1 or 2 Cocorra cut into chunks—about 2 cups

8 chunks of zucchini

1 large onion

8 cherry tomatoes and/or 1 bell pepper, cut into 8 chunks

Toast the cumin and coriander seed in a small, dry frying pan, then grind them in a spice mill, coffee grinder, or with a mortar and pestle. Combine them in a large bowl with salt, paprika and pepper flakes. Tear up the bay leaves and add, along with the garlic, lemon rind and juice and olive oil. Add the chunks of mushroom and zucchini and toss them in the marinade. Allow to marinate overnight.

Peel the onion, cutting off the top and roots, but leaving the base intact. Cut into 8 pieces through the base, so the layers stay together. Alternate the mushrooms on skewers with the zucchini, onion, tomatoes and peppers. Barbeque the kebobs or cook them on a grill or under a broiler, turning to cook all sides, until they are cooked through.

Lamb Saag with Black Trumpets

This dish is also good with winter chanterelles or hedgehogs.

Serves 8

8 tablespoons coconut, peanut or sunflower oil

¼ teaspoon black peppercorns

1 teaspoon cumin seed

1 teaspoon coriander seed

6 cloves

6 cardamom pods

2 bay leaves

2 onions, chopped

6 cloves garlic, peeled and chopped

1 inch piece of ginger, minced or grated

2 pounds lamb, cut into chunks (or ground lamb may be used)

¼ teaspoon cayenne

¼ teaspoon garam masala*

4 cups black trumpets, torn

5 tablespoons yogurt

2 teaspoons salt

2 pounds spinach, fresh or frozen

Put the oil in a large frying pan over medium heat, and sauté the pepper, cumin, coriander, cloves, cardamom (break the pods open and use both the pods and seeds), bay, onions, ginger and garlic until the onions are beginning to brown. Add the meat, cayenne, garam masala and the black trumpets. Turn down to low and cover, simmering for one hour (if ground lamb is used, you may simmer for only 20 minutes, but the flavors of the spices will not be as well melded), stirring occasionally.

Add the yogurt one tablespoon at a time, stirring until it simmers between each addition. Add the salt and spinach, cover and allow spinach to steam for three

---

*Garam masala is an Indian spice blend and can be bought already mixed in most grocery stores.

minutes. Then uncover. If there are excess juices in the pan, turn the heat up to medium-high, and cook, stirring occasionally until the excess water has evaporated. Serve with rice or naan bread.

Mediterranean Lamb Stew with Black Trumpets

Serves 4

½ cup dried black trumpets, or 2 cups fresh

1 pound lamb stew meat

1 onion

2 cups sliced zucchini

½ eggplant

Salt

1 bell pepper

5 cloves garlic, sliced

½ cup raisins

3 cups stock or water

1 (15-ounce) can tomato sauce or 1 (6-ounce) can tomato paste

1 cup white wine

2 bay leaves

1 teaspoon cumin

1 teaspoon cinnamon

1 teaspoon basil

1 tablespoon coriander

½ to 1 jalapeno minced, or 1 to 2 teaspoons red pepper flakes

¼ cup olive oil

Dice the eggplant, salt it thoroughly, and set aside for ½ hour. Rinse and sauté in 2 to 3 tablespoons of the olive oil over medium heat until cooked through.

Set aside.

In a stew pot, sauté the onion, zucchini and lamb in the remaining olive oil until the vegetables are about half done. Add the garlic, cumin, cinnamon, basil, coriander, and jalapeno or red pepper. Sauté a couple of minutes, then add stock, wine and tomato sauce or paste. Stir in the eggplant, black trumpets, bay leaves, bell pepper and raisins. Add salt to taste and bring to a boil. Turn down heat and simmer, covered, about ½ hour or until the lamb is tender. Serve over rice, or a blend of rice and lentils.

African-Style Fruited Fistulina Curry

If you prefer a particular cut, 4 pounds of chicken thighs, breasts, etc. can be substituted for the whole cut-up chicken.

Serves 6

1 chicken, disjointed

3 tablespoons coconut oil

1 onion, chopped

2 cups beefsteak mushroom, diced

3 tablespoons curry powder

½ teaspoon powdered ginger

1 cup chopped fresh apples

½ cup dried apricots

½ cup prunes

¼ cup raisins

1 teaspoon salt

¼ cup lemon juice

½ cup chopped roasted peanuts

In a large non-reactive skillet, sauté the chicken in the coconut oil over medium-high heat, turning the pieces, until they are browned on the surface. Turn the heat down to medium, and remove the chicken to a platter.

In the same pan, sauté the onion and mushroom until the onion is translucent. Add the curry powder, ginger, and add the chicken back in. Toss to coat the chicken with the spices. Add the fruits and salt, and enough water to just cover the curry, and add the lemon juice. Simmer, without a lid, for ½ hour or so, until the chicken is tender and the liquid has thickened. Serve over rice, garnished with peanuts.

African Peanut Stew with Mushrooms

Serves 6

1 eggplant, or 3 cups diced puffballs (if giant, peeled first)

1 chicken, disjointed

3 carrots, cut in chunks

1 onion, chopped

2 cups boletes, sliced and cut into bite-sized pieces

3 tablespoons coconut, peanut or palm oil

2 tablespoons tomato paste

⅔ cup peanut butter

½ teaspoon dried ginger

Pinch of cayenne

2 teaspoons salt

1 (14-ounce) can tomatoes

2 cups kale or spinach, coarsely chopped

If using eggplant, peel if desired, dice, and salt liberally. Allow to sit for 20 minutes, then rinse and drain.

Put the chicken in a stew pot with the carrots and about 2 cups water, cover, and simmer for 20 minutes. Drain off and reserve 1 cup of the broth.

Meanwhile, sauté the onions, mushrooms and eggplant or puffballs in the oil, until the onions are translucent.

In a small bowl, and mix together the tomato paste, peanut butter and seasonings. Mix in, a little at a time, the juice from the can of tomatoes. Mix the resulting slurry into the chicken. Add the sautéed mixture, and the canned tomatoes. Stir in some of the reserved chicken broth, until the sauce is thin enough that it won't burn. Cover, bring to a simmer, and simmer for 15 minutes, adding more broth if necessary to prevent burning. Add the greens, simmer 3 more minutes, and serve.

Matsutake Sukiyaki

Recipe by Christine Schomer. If using meat, it may be sliced more thinly if you partially freeze it before slicing. Sukiyaki is traditionally cooked at the table, which one may do with an electric frying pan. Otherwise, it may be cooked in a large cast-iron frying pan or a wok on the stove.

Serves 4 to 6

2 to 3 cups sliced matsutakes

2 tablespoons peanut oil

1 pound thinly sliced beef or chicken (optional)

1 can bamboo shoots

6 green onions (scallions), coarsely chopped

8 leaves Chinese cabbage, coarsely chopped

1 quart chicken or vegetable broth (unsalted)

2 cups mirin or sake

2 cups soy sauce, or to taste

1 bundle bean thread (cellophane) noodles or yam (konnyaka or shirataki) noodles

Sauté the mushrooms in the peanut oil over medium heat. When they begin to soften, set them aside in a bowl; turn up the heat and brown the meat.

Meanwhile, in a pitcher, combine the broth, wine, soy sauce and the juice from the can of bamboo shoots.

When the meat is browned, push it into a discrete pile to one side of the pan. Leaving an open area in the center of the pan, place the cooked mushrooms in another pile. Put the bamboo shoots in another pile and add the green onions in another. Put the cabbage in another. Pour the broth blend, to just cover the other ingredients, into the hole in the center. Bring to a simmer and add the noodles to the center of the pan. Simmer gently for a minute or two and serve. (Traditionally served with beaten raw egg as a dipping sauce.)

Pumpkin and Mushroom Red Thai Curry

Serves 8 to 12

3 cups chopped boletes, shaggy manes, chanterelles, hedgehogs or matsutakes

2 cups chopped, skinned, and seeded pumpkin (or any other winter squash)

1 onion, chopped

1 cup smoked pig's ears (optional; see recipe on page 255)

2 tablespoons red Thai curry paste

1 can coconut milk

1 tablespoon Thai fish sauce

1 tablespoon soy sauce

1 cup low-salt chicken or vegetable broth

1 cup chopped chicken, pork, beef or tofu

1 tablespoon coconut oil

8 to 16 stalks cilantro

4 limes, quartered

Sauté the onion, mushrooms and meat or tofu in the coconut oil and curry paste until it browns slightly. Add the broth and pumpkin. Cover and simmer until the pumpkin is tender, adding more broth or water only if necessary. Add the soy sauce, fish sauce and coconut milk and simmer, uncovered, until the coconut milk thickens into a nice sauce. Salt to taste and serve over rice or rice noodles. Garnish with cilantro and serve with lime.

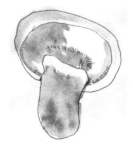

Gamboni Green Curry

This is a Thai-style dish using boletus. Pork or beef may be used instead of chicken.

Serves 4 to 6

2 to 3 red chilies, seeded and stemmed, cut into strips

1 (15-ounce) can coconut milk

2 to 3 fresh gamboni buttons, chopped

½ to ¾ pound chicken or tofu, cut into strips (chicken) or chunks (tofu)

1 to 2 tablespoons green curry paste

2 Kaffir lime leaves (if unavailable, substitute lime peel zest)

½ pound eggplant, diced

2 to 3 summer squash, chopped into 1 inch cubes

1 teaspoon palm sugar (or ½ teaspoon white sugar and ½ teaspoon maple syrup)

1 to 2 tablespoons Thai fish sauce

1 cup fresh basil leaves, stems removed

Salt to taste

Sauté the chilies in 2 tablespoons of the coconut milk until they are fragrant. Reduce the heat and add the mushrooms, chicken, the curry paste, and the rest of the coconut milk. Then add the Kaffir lime or grated lime peel, eggplant, squash, palm sugar, and fish sauce. When the meat is cooked through, add the sweet basil leaves, and salt to taste. Remove from heat, and serve.

Bacon and Chanterelle Soufflé

Serves 4

2 slices thick cut bacon

Butter

1 cup chanterelles

1 clove garlic, minced

4 tablespoons flour

1 cup stock or milk

½ cup cheddar cheese

3 eggs, separated

¼ teaspoon cream of tartar

¼ teaspoon paprika

1 teaspoon minced parsley

Sauté the bacon in a frying pan until crisp. Drain on paper towels. Chop or crumble. Measure the bacon grease by tablespoons into a sauce pan. Add enough butter to make 4 tablespoons total. Set aside.

Chop the chanterelles finely, and sauté in the same frying pan used to cook the bacon. When the chanterelles have exuded their excess water and it has evaporated, add the garlic and sauté 1 minute longer. Set aside.

In a small bowl, beat the egg yolks. In the sauce pan, over medium heat, add 4 tablespoons flour to the fat. Cook and stir until it becomes bubbly, stirring constantly. Add the milk or stock. Bring to a boil stirring constantly, then reduce the heat to a simmer. Stir in the chanterelles, bacon, and cheese. Add the egg yolks to the sauce, stirring constantly for 1 or 2 minutes, until they thicken the sauce. Do not let it boil. Remove from heat. Stir in the paprika and parsley. Cool completely.

Preheat the oven to 325° F. Beat the egg whites, adding the cream of tartar when the eggs get bubbly. Beat until stiff. Fold ⅓ of them into the mushroom mixture, then gently fold in the other ⅔. Pour the soufflé into an ungreased 7-inch soufflé pan and put it in the oven. After 10 minutes, turn the heat up to 350° F and bake another 20 minutes or until it is golden, puffed, and set in the center. Serve immediately.

Smoked Salmon and Chanterelle Savory Cheesecake

May be served as an hors d'oeuvre or a main dish for lunch or dinner.

Makes one 8-inch cheesecake, Serves 12 to 16

½ cup almonds, raw or roasted

½ cup flour or rice flour

2 tablespoons butter

1 tablespoon water

1 to 1½ cups finely chopped fresh chanterelles

1 pound cream cheese, softened

⅓ to ½ pound smoked salmon, shredded

4 green onions, chopped

¼ cup finely chopped red bell pepper

1 cup sour cream

3 eggs, separated

½ teaspoon salt

1 tablespoon lemon juice

Grind the nuts in a blender, food processor, or coffee grinder to a coarse meal consistency. Mix the ground nuts with the flour. Melt the butter and mix it in. Sprinkle on the water and mix it in. Press into the bottom of an 8-inch spring-form pan.

Preheat the oven to 325° F. Dry sauté the chanterelles. If excess water comes out of them, cook them until water has evaporated. Cream the cream cheese and blend in the smoked salmon, chanterelles, onion and chopped red bell pepper. Then stir in the egg yolks, salt, lemon juice, and half of the sour cream. (Reserve the other half to cover the top of the cake after baking.)

Beat the egg whites until they make stiff peaks, and fold them in, gently. Pour the batter over the crust and bake for 45 minutes to 1 hour, until puffy and set to the center, and golden on top. After cooling (it will fall), spread with the remaining sour cream.

Tofu Chanterelle Stir-Fry

Serves 4

1 teaspoon cumin seeds

1 pound firm tofu, drained

1 teaspoon turmeric

1 cup or more fresh chanterelles

1 tablespoon ghee, butter, or oil, or a mixture

Minced fresh garlic (optional)

Tamari

Salt to taste

In a small dry pan, toast 1 teaspoon cumin seeds, tossing and shaking till fragrant. Put the seeds in a coffee grinder or spice mill and grind them coarsely. Set aside.

Cut the tofu into ½ inch cubes and pat dry. Put a teaspoon of turmeric powder in a medium sized bowl and toss the tofu cubes until they turn a nice even yellow all over.

Tear the chanterelles into strips from cap edge to stem by pulling them apart gently. They should separate into thin (⅛-inch) curly strips.

Melt the ghee or butter and/or oil over medium heat and cook the mushrooms until they begin to soften. Toss the cumin and the tofu into the pan and shake the pan gently to mix the mushrooms and the tofu. Add the garlic if using and a tiny splash of tamari and cook over medium heat for 5 minutes or until tofu is heated on all sides. Be careful to shake the pan or just stir the tofu very gently as it tends to crumble and you want the nice yellow cubes to stay more or less whole. The outside of the cubes should be rather dry. Be careful not to add too much tamari to the pan as this will steam the tofu and it will fall apart. Serve with a nice vegetable dish or rice and salad.

Admirable Fruited Stir-fry

Serves 2

1 *Boletus mirabilis*, thinly sliced

1 tablespoon butter, peanut or coconut oil

½ pound pork or chicken meat, diced (optional)

1 cup thinly sliced Chinese cabbage

1 apple sliced

Zest and juice of 1 orange

1 tablespoon soy sauce

½ teaspoon toasted sesame oil

Stir-fry the mushrooms in butter or oil. When about half done, add the meat. Cook a few minutes then add the Chinese cabbage, and apple. Continue to stir-fry until nearly done. Add the orange rind, juice, soy sauce and sesame oil, remove from heat, and serve over rice.

Fruited Beef (or Venison) with Chanterelles

Recipe from Ryane Snow.

This may be made without the meat and served as a side dish.

Serves 4

1 onion, chopped

2 cups chanterelles, torn into pieces

1 tablespoon butter

1 pound tender beef or venison, thinly sliced, or hamburger rolled into meatballs

1 cup sherry

2 pears or apples

1 cup huckleberries

Salt to taste

Sauté the onions and chanterelles in the butter. Add the meat when the onions get translucent. Sauté, stirring, until the meat is slightly browned. Add the sherry and pear or apple; cover, and simmer for 15 minutes. Remove lid and simmer until juices are reduced to a sauce. Stir in huckleberries and serve over rice, quinoa, or millet.

Sweet and Sour Pork with Beefsteak Mushroom

The tartness of the Fistulina *fits well in this recipe.*

Serves 4 to 6

1 pound boneless pork, sliced thin

1 onion, chopped

2 to 3 cups beefsteak mushroom, chopped

1 carrot, sliced

1 teaspoon finely chopped ginger

1 tablespoon butter or oil (peanut or coconut)

1 bell pepper, chopped

1 (8-ounce) can diced pineapple

1 cup chicken, pork or vegetable broth

2 tablespoons brown sugar, or to taste

1 tablespoon rice vinegar, or to taste

1 tablespoon soy sauce, or to taste

½ teaspoon salt, or to taste

1 tablespoon cornstarch

Stir-fry the pork, onion, carrot, ginger and mushroom in butter or oil until the onion is translucent and the pork is cooked. Add the bell pepper and pineapple (reserving the juice), and sauté a few minutes more. Add the broth, sugar, vinegar, soy sauce, and salt to taste. Mix the cornstarch into the reserved pineapple juice. When the sweet and sour pork comes to a boil, add the cornstarch mixture. Stir constantly as it thickens and comes to a boil again. Remove from heat and serve over rice.

Double Lemon Chicken

This dish is actually much milder on the lemon than Chinese lemon chicken, using no lemon juice but only lemon slices, so that the lemon flavor of the Boletus mirabilis *is not overpowered, but contrasts nicely with the tangy slices of lemon.*

Serves 4

1 large *Boletus mirabilis*

1 medium onion

1 pound boned chicken, sliced thinly

1 tablespoon butter

1 tablespoon sesame seeds (optional)

1 lemon, Meyer if possible

1 cup stock or water

1 tablespoon cornstarch

1 tablespoon soy sauce

2 tablespoons lemon juice

1 tablespoon sugar

Chop the onion and slice the mushroom. Sauté them in the butter with the chicken, in a non-cast-iron pan. (If the chicken is already cooked, add it at the end of the sautéing.)

Toast the sesame seeds in a dry frying pan while the onions are cooking. When the seeds are brown, remove them to a dish to cool so they do not burn. Set aside for later.

Slice the lemon thinly, crosswise, peel and all. Remove any seeds. When the onions are translucent and golden add the lemons and sauté a few minutes longer. Mix the stock or water, soy sauce, cornstarch, lemon juice and sugar together, and add to the mushroom mixture, stirring constantly as the sauce thickens and comes to a boil. Serve immediately over rice, garnished with the sesame seeds.

Coriander Prawns with Black Trumpets

Serves 4

1 pound prawns

1 tablespoon lemon juice

1 teaspoon coriander seed

1 teaspoon cumin seed

1 teaspoon oregano

1 to 2 tablespoons butter

1 to 2 tablespoons coconut oil or sesame oil

1½ cups sliced black trumpets

6 cloves garlic, sliced

2 cups chopped cilantro leaf and some stem

¼ cup dry cooking sherry

Salt to taste

Wash, pat dry, peel and de-vein the prawns, and put them in a bowl. Squeeze some lemon juice over them and toss.

In a small frying pan dry toast the cumin and the coriander seeds until fragrant. Remove from heat and grind in a spice grinder, mortar and pestle, or blender. Place in a bowl with the oregano and mix the spices well. Roll the prawns in the spice-herb mixture to coat.

Heat the oil and butter in a heavy cast iron skillet. Add the mushrooms and the garlic and stir for a minute over medium heat. Add the prawns and cook on one side about 3 minutes or until pink when flipped over. Turn each prawn over, stir a little, and add the 2 cups chopped cilantro. Add a dash of sherry, a sprinkle of salt, and stir a minute more. Cover the pan, and let cook another 2 to 3 minutes until prawns are just cooked through. It's important not to overcook prawns. If they are more than half done when you turn them, just toss them with the cilantro and cover the pan, turning off the flame and letting them all steam together to wilt the greens without overdoing the prawns. Serve over rice.

Matsutake Tempura

Things that make for the most crisp tempura are coldness of the batter, not over-mixing the batter, and proper oil temperature. Be sure to fry only a few pieces at a time, so the mushroom slices do not cool the oil too much.

Serves 3 to 6

2 to 3 large, open, juicy matsutakes

1 egg

1 cup ice water or chilled soda water

1 cup all purpose flour, sifted

Oil for deep fat frying

¼ cup soy sauce

¼ cup mirin or sherry

1 tablespoon brown sugar or 2 tablespoons candy cap syrup (see recipe on page 219)

¼ teaspoon sesame oil

Slice the matsutakes about ¼ inch thick. Heat the oil in a wok or large frying pan.

Meanwhile, make the batter: beat the egg and ice water until they are well-mixed. Stir in the flour, quickly. Do not over mix or the batter will be less crisp.

Prepare the dipping sauce: combine the soy sauce, mirin, sugar and sesame oil in a small bowl.

When the oil reaches 170° F, or when a drop of batter sinks half-way and then rises to the top of the oil, begin frying the tempura. Dip the mushroom slices in the batter and fry them about 1 minute on each side, or until they become a light golden color. Drain them on paper towels or on a rack and serve immediately with the dipping sauce.

Drinks

Candy Cap Ice Cream Soda

Serves 2

⅓ cup candy cap syrup (see recipe on page 219)

4 scoops vanilla or candy cap ice cream

12 ounces club soda or seltzer water

Divide the candy cap syrup between 2 tall glasses. Put two scoops of ice cream in each glass. Fill with soda water. Enjoy.

Candy Cap Milk or Nightcap

Serves 1

8 ounces milk

2 tablespoons candy cap syrup (see recipe on page 219)

2 tablespoons brandy (optional—for the nightcap version)

You may heat the milk or use it cold. Stir in the syrup (and brandy if desired) and enjoy!

Candy Cap Peanut Butter Smoothie or Protein Drink

If using banana or a sweetened protein powder in this recipe, decrease the candy cap syrup to 2 teaspoons, or to taste.

Serves 1

1 cup milk

2 tablespoons peanut butter

1 tablespoon candy cap syrup (see recipe on page 219)

½ teaspoon cinnamon

½ banana (optional)

1 egg (optional)

2 tablespoons protein powder (optional)

Put all ingredients into a blender and puree. Serve immediately.

Candy Cap Milkshake or Malt

Serves 2 to 3

¾ cup milk

2 tablespoons candy cap syrup (see recipe on page 219)

2 teaspoons malt powder (optional)

1½ to 2 cups ice cream—vanilla, caramel or peanut butter

Put the milk, syrup, and malt powder (if using) in a blender and blend to mix. Add the ice cream ½ cup at a time until desired thickness is attained. Pour into glasses and serve.

Candy Cap Cantaloupe Agua Fresca or Smoothie

For smoothie, skip the draining and just blend all ingredients.

Serves 4

1 cantaloupe

1 tablespoon lemon juice

¼ to ⅜ cup candy cap syrup (see recipe on page 219)

¼ teaspoon cinnamon (optional)

Halve and seed the cantaloupe. Scoop the flesh of one half into a blender. Add 1 cup of water and puree.

Line a large sieve or colander with cheesecloth and set it into a bowl. Pour puree in and let drain. Squeeze cheesecloth to get all the juice out. Repeat process with the other half of the cantaloupe. Stir in lemon, cinnamon, and candy cap syrup to taste. Ladle into glasses with ice.

V-9 Juice

Serves 2

1 (12-ounce) bottle V-8 juice

2 tablespoons dried boletes, or smoked dried boletes

Purée dried mushrooms in a blender with the V-8 juice. May be garnished with a wedge of lime or lemon, a stalk of celery, or an olive on a toothpick (or see recipe for hedgehog garnishes on page 54). May be served with or without ice.

Hot Candy Cap Cider

Serves 4

10 candy caps fresh or dried

1 quart apple cider

1 stick cinnamon

Purée the mushrooms in the blender with half the cider. Put it in a saucepan with the remaining cider and the cinnamon. Bring to a boil, simmer for 5 minutes and serve. May be garnished with a sprinkle of nutmeg.

Candy Cap Chai Tea

You may make a simpler version by using chai tea bags and adding one candy cap mushroom per tea bag.

Makes 1 quart

3 bags or 1 tablespoon black tea

1 stick cinnamon

3 cardamom pods

1 whole clove

1 thin slice fresh ginger

3 candy caps, fresh or dried

2 cups milk

1 tablespoon sugar, or other sweetening to taste

Put the spices and candy caps into a saucepan with 2¼ cups water. Bring to a boil, turn down to a simmer and cover. Simmer for 15 minutes. Turn off burner, add tea and steep for 5 minutes. Strain. Pour tea back into pan, add milk and sugar and reheat to drinking temperature.

Candy Cap Herbal Chai (bulk)

This is a quite good herbal chai. The recipe is by weight, not volume. The base is a roasted, malted barley, which may be purchased as a beer making supply, or you may make your own with whole unpolished (not pearled) barley. Sprout it in a sprouting jar for 3 to 5 days, until roots begin to form. Then toast it in a dry frying pan, stirring constantly, until it is medium brown. The toasted barley should be ground in small batches in a blender or other grinding device until it is the coarseness of bulgur or oat groats.

Makes about 1½ pounds bulk dry tea

10 ounces malted, roasted barley, coarsely ground

2 ounces chamomile

10 ounces broken cinnamon or cassia bark

2 ounces dried ginger

1 ounce cardamom pods, crushed

⅓ ounce cloves

1 ounce chopped dried candy caps

1 tablespoon chili flakes (optional)

Mix all ingredients thoroughly. To brew the tea, use 3 tablespoons tea blend per quart of water. Bring to a boil and simmer, covered, 10 to 15 minutes. Strain the tea, pressing as much liquid as possible out of the grounds. Add 2 cups milk per quart of tea, sweeten to taste, and reheat to serving temperature.

Boletus Chai

This is a robust chai, which needs less sweetening than some of the more desserty chais. It is good served with a hearty meal. For an herbal version, substitute rooibos, honeybush, red clover, chamomile or another herbal base for the black tea.

Makes 6 cups

4 large slices dried *Boletus edulis*

1 stick cinnamon

1-inch piece of fresh ginger, sliced thinly

4 cardamom pods, crushed

6 cloves

1 bay leaf

1 teaspoon cumin seed

1-inch piece fresh turmeric, thinly sliced, or ½ teaspoon powdered

2 tablespoons black tea, or herbal tea base

2 cups milk

1 tablespoon honey or to taste

Put all ingredients except the tea, milk and honey in a large saucepan with 5 cups water, and bring to a boil. Simmer, lidded, for ½ hour. Add the tea, remove from heat and steep for 5 minutes. Strain. Return liquid to pot, add 2 cups milk and the honey. Reheat to drinking temperature and serve.

Turkey Tail Chai

This is good to drink anytime, but tastes particularly good if you're sick.

Makes 6 cups

12 turkey tails, coarsely chopped

2-inch piece fresh ginger, sliced

1 stick cinnamon

12 cloves

1 bay leaf

1 teaspoon rosemary

1-inch piece fresh turmeric, sliced or ½ teaspoon dried

Pinch crushed dried red pepper

½ teaspoon grated lemon rind

2 tablespoons chamomile, red clover, rooibos or black tea

1 cup milk or milk substitute

2 tablespoons honey

2 tablespoons turkey tail elixir (optional)

The night before, put the mushrooms in a large sauce pan, and add 6 cups water. Bring to a boil, turn down and simmer, lidded, for ½ hour. Let sit overnight.

The next day, add the spices, including the lemon rind, and simmer, lidded, for another half hour. Add the tea, remove from heat and allow to steep for 5 minutes. Strain. Add milk, honey and elixir, and serve. If it will not all be served at once, add milk, honey and elixir to each cup, so the tea may be stored in the refrigerator without souring.

Hot Mulled Candy Cap Tea Punch

Makes 2 to 2½ quarts

20 dried or fresh candy caps

4 teaspoons loose leaf black tea or 4 tea bags

1 quart water

2 cups apple juice

2 cups orange juice

1 cinnamon stick

2 cloves

1 pint brandy or rum (optional)

Nutmeg

Put 1 quart water, the candy caps, cinnamon, and cloves in a large pot with lid. Bring to a boil and simmer for 15 minutes.

Remove from heat. Add the black tea. Steep an additional 15 minutes. Strain. Add apple and orange juice and reheat to hot but not boiling. Add alcohol if desired. For a cold punch, omit reheating and chill instead. Ladle into cups and top each with grated nutmeg when serving.

Mulled Wine with Candy Caps

For a sweeter version, replace the candy caps with ¼ cup candy cap syrup (see recipe on page 219).

Makes about 3 cups

10 dried candy caps,

1 (750-milliliter) bottle sweet red, rosé or white wine

1 stick of cinnamon

2 cloves

Sugar (optional)

1 orange, sliced thinly with skin left on (organic recommended)

Put the wine in a pot with the mushrooms, cinnamon, cloves, and orange slices. Heat to quite warm, but not hot enough to simmer. Put lid on pot, remove from heat and let it mull for a couple of hours to overnight. Sweeten to taste, if desired. When ready to serve, heat to a good warm temperature but do not boil. Serve warm.

Candy Cap Cranberry Orange Punch

Makes about 3½ quarts

2 cups cranberry juice

2 cups orange juice

½ cup candy cap syrup (see recipe on page 219)

1 liter ginger ale

1 liter seltzer water

1 pint raspberry sherbet, or ice cubes

1 cup brandy or dark rum (optional)

1 orange, thinly sliced into rings for garnish (optional)

Mix together the juices and the syrup in a gallon punch bowl or pitcher. Add the sodas and sherbet or ice, and brandy if using, float orange slices on top, and serve.

Candy Cap Piña Colada Punch

The coconut milk in this punch makes a lasting froth with the addition of the seltzer water.

Makes 1 to 1¼ gallons

4 cups pineapple juice

2 cup orange, tangerine or mango juice

1 (12-ounce) can coconut cream or a good-quality coconut milk

½ cup candy cap syrup (see recipe on page 219)

2 liters seltzer water

1 cup dark rum (optional)

1 pint orange sherbet or ice

In a large punch bowl, put the pineapple and orange juice, and mix in the coconut cream with a wire whisk. Add the candy cap syrup and rum. Just before serving, float the sherbet or ice in the punch, and pour in the seltzer water.

Matsutake Sake

Recipe from Ryane Snow

Makes 750 milliliters

1 (750-milliliter) bottle of sake

¼ cup minced matsutake mushroom

Pour the sake into a quart bottle. Add the matsutake. Age at least a week, and up to a month or more. When the flavor is strong enough, strain out the mushrooms, which can be used in cooking, and pour the sake back into its bottle. Serve warm or cold.

Candy Cap Brandy

You may make this mildly sweet, just enough to taste the candy cap, or add more sugar to make a cordial.

1 (750-milliliter) bottle of brandy (rum or whiskey may be used)

½ cup fresh or ¼ cup dried candy caps, coarsely chopped

½ to 1 cup sugar, or more, to taste

Put all ingredients into a quart jar and allow to age a couple of weeks to several months. Candy caps may be strained out, or left in the jar.

Alternatively, you may decant about a cup of brandy from the brandy bottle, stuff the mushrooms down the neck of the bottle, pour the sugar in with a funnel, and refill the bottle with brandy.

Spiced Rum with Candy Caps

Makes 750 milliliters

10 fresh or dried candy caps

1 (750-milliliter) bottle of dark rum

1 inch of cinnamon stick

1 clove

2 cardamom pods

1 thin slice of fresh ginger

Pinch of nutmeg

1 (2-inch) strip of lemon rind (pare thinly to avoid the white part)

¼ to ½ cup sugar, to taste

In a quart bottle, combine the rum, mushrooms, rind and spices. Let sit 3 to 5 days. Add sugar to taste. Mushrooms, rind and spices may be strained out when flavor is strong enough, or may be left in the bottle for decoration.

Candy Cap Liqueur

Makes 750 milliliters

1 (750-milliliter) bottle of vodka

1 cup fresh or ½ cup dried candy caps

2 to 3 cups sugar, to taste

Put all ingredients into a quart jar and allow to age for several months. Candy caps may be strained out or left in for decoration.

Candy Cap Eggnog

This eggnog is incredibly delicious, with or without brandy.

Serves 2

2 eggs

¼ to ⅓ cup candy cap syrup (see recipe on page 219)

2 tablespoons to ½ cup brandy (optional)

1 cup half-and-half

Nutmeg or mace

Put the eggs, syrup, brandy and half-and-half in a blender. Vary the ingredients, depending on whether you prefer your eggnog sweeter or less sweet, or weak or strong on the alcohol. Add a pinch of nutmeg. Blend. Pour it into two glasses, and garnish with a sprinkle of nutmeg.

Candy Cap Old Fashioned

Serves 1

¼ cup bourbon whiskey

1 teaspoon candy cap syrup (see recipe on page 219)

¼ cup or more club soda (optional)

Mix together the whiskey and syrup; serve over ice, with club soda if desired.

Candy Cap Daiquiri

Serves 1

1 teaspoon candy cap syrup (see recipe on page 219)

¼ cup rum

¼ cup ice

Mix together the rum and syrup, and serve over ice.

Hot Candy Cap Toddy

Serves 1

¼ cup bourbon whiskey

¼ cup hot water

1 teaspoon candy cap syrup (see recipe on page 219)

Mix together all ingredients and serve immediately

Pineapple Candy Cap Mojito

Makes 8 servings

1 cup candy cap syrup (see recipe on page 219)

Half of a fresh pineapple

2 limes, each cut into 8 wedges

2 cups light or dark rum

Club soda, to taste

8 candied candy caps for garnish (optional; see recipe on page 250)

Cut the pineapple half into two quarters. Starting with one quarter, cut out the core and cut the flesh into chunks. Put them in a blender with the candy cap syrup and puree. Cut the other pineapple quarter into chunks, also.

For each cocktail, combine 2 lime wedges, 2 to 3 chunks of pineapple, ¼ cup rum and ¼ cup candy cap-pineapple puree in a cocktail shaker. Fill with ice and shake vigorously. Pour into a glass and dilute with club soda as desired. Garnish with a candied candy cap.

Turkey Tail Elixir

This is a very strong elixir which may be taken by the spoonful, or mixed with water or vegetable juice, used for martinis, or added to soups.

Makes 1 pint (serving size: 1 teaspoon)

1 pint vodka or gin

12 turkey tail mushrooms

1 4-inch sprig rosemary

2 4-inch sprigs oregano

2 tablespoons fresh thyme

2 tablespoons honey (optional)

Combine all ingredients in a lidded jar. Allow to steep for a month. May be strained if desired, or the herbs and mushrooms left in, to continue to strengthen.

Turkey Tail Martini

Serves 1

1 tablespoon dry vermouth

1 tablespoon dry gin

2 tablespoons turkey tail elixir

Serve over ice and garnish with olive-flavored hedgehog garnishes (see recipe on page 54).

Bloody Beefsteak Cocktail

This is a variation of a Bloody Mary.

Serves 2 to 3

¼ cup diced beefsteak mushroom

1 teaspoon olive oil

1½ cup tomato or V-8 juice

½ cup vodka or turkey tail elixer (see recipe above)

Dash of Worcestershire sauce

Dash of Tabasco sauce

Pinch of salt

2 to 3 stalks of celery, wedges of lemon, or hedgehog garnishes (see recipe on page 54)

Sauté the mushroom in the olive oil in a small frying pan over medium heat until it is tender. Put it into a blender with the tomato juice, vodka, salt and Worcestershire sauce. Add a dash of Tabasco. Blend until smooth. Pour into glasses with ice, garnish and serve.

Smoky Mary Cocktail

This is a variation on a Bloody Mary.

Serves 2 to 3

1½ cups tomato, V-8, or V-9 juice (see recipe on page 205)

½ cup vodka or turkey tail elixir (see recipe on page 216)

¼ cup lemon juice

1 teaspoon powdered smoked wild mushrooms (see recipe on page 255)

¼ teaspoon powdered dried kelp, dulse, or other seaweed (optional)

Pinch of salt

Dash of Worcestershire sauce

Pinch of chipotle powder

2 to 3 stalks of celery or hedgehog garnishes (see recipe on page 54)

Mix all ingredients except the garnishes together in a blender or with a wire whisk. Serve over ice, with celery or hedgehogs.

Candy Cap Paradise Cocktail

Serves 4

⅜ cup gin

½ cup apricot brandy

2 tablespoons candy cap syrup (see recipe on page 219)

¾ cup cracked ice

Shake all ingredients with cracked ice and serve.

Hot Buttered Rum with Candy Cap

Serves 1

1 teaspoon candy cap syrup (see recipe on page 219)

¼ cup dark rum

1 teaspoon butter

Boiling water

Pinch of nutmeg

Put the syrup and rum in a mug. Top with the butter. Fill with boiling water and sprinkle with nutmeg. Serve immediately.

Desserts

Candy Cap Syrup

This is an alternative way to preserve candy caps. It's a key ingredient in many of the following recipes. Syrup will keep, refrigerated, for many months. It may also be sealed in canning jars if made in quantity. While it may be made with dried candy caps, fresh ones give a smoother, better quality syrup.

Syrup has many uses: over pancakes, French toast or ice cream, blended with yogurt or cottage cheese, mixed with soda water (1 to 2 tablespoons per cup) for candy cap sodas, mixed into punches or alcoholic drinks, used as ingredient in candy cap eggnog or candy cap pecan pie, added to smoothies or milk shakes, and as a flavoring for ice cream. It can also be added to fruit salad dressing, may be used in gelatin desserts, and to make mousses.

Makes about 1½ cups

1 cup sugar

1 cup water

½ cup chopped, fresh candy caps, or ¼ cup dried, packed

Purée fresh candy caps and water in blender. (If using dried, see below.) Add to sugar in saucepan. Heat over medium heat, stirring occasionally, until boiling. Turn down to low heat and simmer 5 minutes.

For dried candy caps: soak the mushrooms in the liquid (1 cup water) overnight. Blend, then place in saucepan and add sugar, and boil as above. Strain out solids if desired, but it's not necessary.

Candy Cap Agave Syrup

Recipe by Anna Moore. Amounts of ingredients can be varied according to taste. This concoction can be added to almost any savory or sweet dish in small amounts as a flavoring. It is a great topping on ice cream. This may also be used as a lower glycemic substitute for candy cap syrup in the recipes in this book.

Makes 1½ cups

1 cup dark agave syrup

½ cup Ginger People's ginger syrup

10 to 20 dried candy caps, crushed or powdered

Bring the agave syrup to a low boil and add the candy caps; let cook at least 20 minutes or longer but the more concentrated it becomes the harder it is to pour. Add the ginger syrup and continue to boil for a few minutes. Pour into a clean glass syrup bottle. You can strain out the mushroom fragments but it is not necessary.

Candy Cap Honey

This may be used in any way you would use regular honey. The candy cap flavor is less prominent than with candy cap syrup, but it blends deliciously with the honey flavor, and it is spreadable.

Makes 2 cups

¼ cup fresh candy caps, packed, or ⅛ cup dried

2 cups honey

Put the candy caps in the blender with ¼ cup water. If the mushrooms are dried, use hot water and let them soak a half-hour to soften. Purée the mushrooms.

Put the honey into a small saucepan, and add the mushrooms. Bring to a simmer. Simmer, uncovered, stirring occasionally for 20 to 30 minutes, until it has boiled down to a pint. Watch it carefully to be sure it doesn't boil over.

Candy cap honey will keep well for many months.

Sweet Candy Cap Applesauce

This is excellent topped with candy cap whipped cream.

Serves 4
¼ cup candy cap syrup (see recipe on page 219)
3 apples
1 tablespoon raisins
½ teaspoon cinnamon
¼ teaspoon cardamom
1 tablespoon brandy (optional)

Core and chop the apples. (Peel first if desired.) Put the apples, raisins, and cinnamon in a small saucepan and pour in the candy cap syrup. Cover and bring to a boil. Turn down to low heat and simmer 10 to 15 minutes, until the apples are soft, checking occasionally and adding a little water if necessary to prevent burning. (If cover is tight and heat is low, addition of water should not be necessary). When done, mash the apples with a fork and stir in the brandy. Serve warm or cold.

Candy Cap Baked Pears

Serves 4
2 pears, firm but ripe
4 dried apricots
4 almonds
1 teaspoon minced candied ginger
½ teaspoon powdered ginger
4 teaspoons candy cap syrup (see recipe on page 219)

Preheat the oven to 350° F. Cut the pears in half lengthwise. Scoop out the cores. Mince the dried apricots and almonds and mix together with the candied ginger. Stuff this mixture into the centers of the pears. Put them in a baking dish. Drizzle a spoonful of candy cap syrup over each half. Sprinkle with powdered ginger. Bake for about 30 minutes or until tender. Excellent served plain, with cream, or a la mode.

Candy Cap Baked Apples

Serves 4

4 apples

2 tablespoons raisins

1 teaspoon butter

4 teaspoons candy cap syrup (see recipe on page 219)

Cinnamon

Preheat the oven to 350° F. Core the apples. Stuff the centers with raisins, leaving the top ½ inch unstuffed. Stand the apples in a baking dish. Put ¼ teaspoon butter in each apple well, and drizzle 1 teaspoon candy cap syrup into the well and down the sides. Sprinkle with cinnamon. Bake about 30 minutes, or until tender.

Cantaloupe Candy Cap Delight

Serves 2

1 small cantaloupe

2 scoops vanilla ice cream or candy cap ice cream

2 tablespoons candy cap syrup (see recipe on page 219)

Halve the cantaloupe and scoop out the seeds. Fill the cavity with a scoop of ice cream and top with candy cap syrup.

Candy Cap Pecan Chocolate Chip Cookies

Makes about 4 dozen 2-inch cookies

½ cup butter

2 tablespoons dried ground or ½ cup fresh chopped candy caps

⅓ cup sugar

1 egg

1 teaspoon apple cider vinegar

1¼ cup pecans

1 cup flour

1 tablespoon cinnamon

½ teaspoon salt

½ teaspoon baking soda

1 cup chocolate chips

Preheat the oven to 350° F. Melt the butter with the candy caps (just warm them, don't cook them). Stir in the sugar, egg, and vinegar. Grind ½ cup of the pecans in the blender, to a mealy consistency. Mix the pecan meal, flour, cinnamon, salt and baking soda together and stir into the sugar-butter mixture.

Coarsely chop the remaining pecans and fold in along with the chocolate chips. Put teaspoonfuls on a cookie sheet about 2 inches apart. Bake for about 10 to 15 minutes, until just starting to turn golden near the bottom. Tops may be a little soft still, but not too soft. Cool and enjoy!

Candy Cap Peanut Butter Cookies

These are also excellent with a cup of chocolate chips folded in along with the peanuts.

Makes about 2 dozen 2-inch cookies

½ cup butter

¾ cup brown sugar

1 cup peanut butter

1 egg

1 teaspoon cinnamon

½ teaspoon salt

2 teaspoons vinegar or 2 tablespoons yogurt

1 cup roasted shelled peanuts

½ cup fresh candy caps or ⅓ cup dried

1¼ cup flour

½ teaspoon baking soda

1 cup chocolate chips (optional)

Preheat the oven to 350° F. Cream the butter with the sugar. Cream in the peanut butter. Stir in the egg, cinnamon, salt and vinegar or yogurt. If the candy caps are fresh, mince them and blend them in.

Grind half of the peanuts with any dried mushrooms in a small food processor, blender or grinder to a coarse grind, and add to the batter, blending well. Stir the flour and baking soda together, and mix into the dough. Then stir in the remaining ½ cup whole peanuts, and the chocolate chips, if using.

Roll spoons of the dough into balls, place on cookie sheet and flatten, leaving at least an inch of space between them as they will spread. If desired, gently press the back of a fork into the top of each cookie to make patterns. Bake about 15 minutes, or until tops are no longer soft.

Huckleberry Pancake Cookies

These cookies taste like huckleberry pancakes with maple syrup. This recipe uses frozen huckleberries as fresh ones will smash in the stiff dough and you'll wind up with pink cookies with skins rather than golden cookies with whole berries! Berries should be frozen raw and dry, so they won't stick together. Do not thaw! The cold berries will stiffen the dough up, when added.

Makes about 3 dozen 2-inch cookies

½ cup butter

½ cup brown sugar

2 tablespoons ground dried candy caps

1 egg

½ teaspoon salt

1 teaspoon vinegar

1 teaspoon cinnamon

1⅛ cups flour

½ teaspoon baking soda

1 cup huckleberries (frozen)

Preheat the oven to 350° F. Melt the butter. Stir in the brown sugar, candy caps and the egg. Add the salt, vinegar, and cinnamon. Stir the baking soda into the flour, then fold it into the batter to make a soft dough. Stir in the huckleberries quickly, as they will stiffen the dough. Put onto cookie sheets by the teaspoonful, about 2 inches apart. Bake about 10 minutes, or until brown around the edges and soft, but not gooey, in the centers.

Candy Cap Shortbread

Makes about 2 dozen, depending on size and thickness of cookies

½ cup powdered sugar

1 cup butter, softened

2 tablespoons powdered dried candy caps

2 cups flour

½ cup ground almonds (optional)

¼ cup salt

¼ teaspoon baking powder

Preheat the oven to 375° F. Cream the butter, then cream in the sugar. Blend in the candy caps. Mix together the remaining dry ingredients and work them into the butter mixture with a fork, a wooden spoon or your hands. Roll the dough out, ¼ to ½ inch thick, and cut into squares or cut with a cookie cutter. Bake for about 20 minutes or until beginning to brown on the edges.

Chocolate Candy Cap Nut Bars

Makes 32 (1-inch by 2-inch) bars

Cookie Crust:

½ cup butter

½ cup sugar

1¼ cups flour

¼ teaspoon salt

¼ teaspoon baking powder

½ cup almonds or hazelnuts, ground in food processor or blender

Chocolate Ganache:

½ cup whipping cream

12 ounces bittersweet chocolate, chopped

2 cups toasted macadamia nuts or cashews, lightly salted

Candy Cap Topping:

2 eggs

1 cup candy cap syrup (see recipe on page 219)

½ cup whipping cream

¼ cup butter

1½ cups shredded coconut

Preheat the oven to 350° F, and grease an 8-inch square baking pan. To prepare the crust: cream the butter and sugar; blend in the flour, salt, baking powder and nuts to make a crumbly dough. Press the dough into the bottom of the prepared pan, bringing the crust a half-inch up the sides. Bake 20 minutes. Remove the crust from the oven, and turn off the oven.

Next, prepare the chocolate ganache: heat the whipping cream to a simmer in a small saucepan; remove from heat. Stir in the chocolate until it melts and is smooth. Pour the ganache onto crust. Sprinkle the nuts over the chocolate ganache in an even layer.

Lastly, prepare the topping: beat the eggs in a small bowl, and set aside. Put the syrup and cream into a saucepan. Heat over medium-low heat, stirring constantly with a whisk, until mixture comes to a boil. Stir in the butter. Simmer, stirring, for 10 minutes. Remove from heat and whisk the eggs in quickly. Return to low heat, and stirring constantly with a whisk, reheat to just below a simmer. Pour over the nut and ganache layer. Sprinkle coconut over the top and press in lightly. Chill. Cut when cool and remove the pieces with a spatula.

Mushroom Meringues

I recommend baking on greased parchment paper, as they are hard to get off the pan, even when well-greased. When cool, store in an air-tight container, as they absorb water from the air and get chewy in an hour or so in coastal humidity. If they begin to get sticky, they may be put in a food dehydrator or warm oven and crisped up.

Makes about 2 to 3 dozen

3 egg whites

⅛ teaspoon salt

½ teaspoon cream of tartar

4 tablespoons candy cap syrup (see recipe on page 219)

¼ to ⅜ cup sugar

Preheat the oven to 225° F. Combine the egg whites, salt and cream of tartar. Beat until stiff but not dry. Beat in the syrup, then add the sugar to taste, sprinkling it lightly over the surface and folding it in. The batter may be dropped by the spoonful onto greased parchment paper on a cookie sheet, or you may use a cake decorating kit or paper cone to pipe mushroom shapes onto the paper. Bake 1 to 1½ hours, or until dry and crispy.

Princely Pudding

½ cup chopped *Agaricus augustus*

1 tablespoon butter

2½ cups milk

1 egg

¼ to ½ cup sugar, to taste

¼ teaspoon cinnamon

pinch of cardamom

3 tablespoons cornstarch

Sauté the mushroom in the butter, until it has softened and is cooked through, but is not browned. Combine the cooked mushroom, 2¼ cups of the milk, the egg, sugar and spices, in a blender. Puree. Pour the liquid into a saucepan, and warm it, stirring frequently. As it becomes hot, stir constantly, until it thickens slightly from the egg.

Then combine the remaining ¼ cup milk with the cornstarch, and add it, stirring constantly until the pudding thickens and comes to a simmer. Turn heat to low and simmer, stirring constantly, for one minute. Remove from heat, cool, and serve.

Candy Cap Pudding

This recipe is also excellent with anise clitocybes in place of the candy caps. Use ½ cup fresh, and mince them, or run them through the blender with the milk and egg.

Serves 6

3 cups milk (may use part cream or half-and-half for a richer pudding)

1 egg

⅓ cup sugar

¼ cup cornstarch

3 tablespoons dried ground candy caps

1 tablespoon butter (optional)

Pinch of salt

Mix the cornstarch with ¼ cup of water and set aside.

Beat the eggs and beat in the milk with a wire whisk or fork (or blend them briefly in a blender, with the mushrooms). Stir in the sugar and the mushrooms.

Heat the milk blend to a simmer, in a saucepan over a low flame, stirring constantly with a wire whisk. Stir the cornstarch and water mixture and add it quickly, while stirring, to the simmering milk blend. Continue stirring constantly until it returns to a simmer. Allow it to simmer, while stirring, for one minute. Remove the pudding from the heat and stir in the butter. Cool before serving. May also be used as a pie filling.

Candy Cap Butterscotch Pudding

This is a sweeter pudding than the previous recipe. You may cut the sugar if you wish, but it needs quite a bit of sugar for a butterscotch flavor.

Makes 8 servings

⅜ cup cornstarch

3½ cups milk (for a richer pudding use part cream or half and half)

¼ cup butter

¾ cup brown sugar

2 tablespoons dried ground candy caps

1 egg

In a small bowl, stir the cornstarch into ½ cup of the milk. Beat in the egg. Set aside.

Melt the butter in a medium-sized saucepan. Cook gently until it begins to brown. Add the brown sugar and stir until the sugar melts. Stir in the remaining 3 cups of milk and the candy caps. Heat over low-medium heat stirring frequently, until it simmers.

Stir the cornstarch mixture to blend and then add it to the hot milk, stirring constantly with a wire whisk. Continue to heat as the pudding thickens, until it begins to boil. Turn burner down and simmer, stirring constantly, for one minute. Remove from heat and cool before serving.

Candy Cap Tapioca

Serves 6

3 cups milk

2 eggs separated

¼ cup fresh chopped (or 2 tablespoons dried) candy caps

¼ cup sugar

¼ cup quick cooking tapioca

¼ teaspoon salt

Purée the milk with the egg yolks, mushrooms, salt, and sugar in the blender. Transfer to a 2 quart saucepan, stir in the tapioca. Let stand 5 minutes to soften. Meanwhile beat the egg whites until stiff.

Bring the tapioca mixture to a rolling boil, stirring frequently. Remove from heat. Fold in ⅓ of the egg whites, then fold in the rest of the whites. Cool and serve.

Anise Clitocybe Tapioca

Follow the above instructions, substituting ½ cup fresh anise clitocybe for the candy caps.

Candy Cap or Anise Clitocybe Custard

Serves 8

1 quart milk (may use part half-and-half for richer custard)

4 eggs

¼ to ⅓ cup sugar (to taste)

½ cup candy caps or ¾ cup anise clitocybe

Preheat the oven to 325° F. Put the mushrooms, eggs, sugar, plus 2 cups milk in the blender, and blend until pureed. Pour into an 8-inch square baking dish. Stir in the rest of the milk.

Set the custard pan in a larger baking dish, and fill the outside dish with boiling water. (The water should be deep enough to come about halfway up the outside of the custard pan.) Put the whole contraption into the oven. Bake for about 45 minutes to an hour or until set in the center. If the custard begins to boil, turn down the oven to 275° F in order to prevent it separating.

Candy Cap Flan

Use an 8-inch-square glass baking pan for this recipe; it does not need to be greased. Prepare a larger pan that the 8-inch pan will sit in by putting the baking pan into the larger pan, then pouring boiling water into the larger pan to fill it one inch. Remove the smaller pan and place the larger pan into the oven.

Serves 8

¾ cup sugar

4 cups milk or half-and-half

20 candy caps, fresh or dried

4 eggs

Preheat the oven to 325° F. Prepare pans as in the notes above. Melt ½ cup of the sugar in a frying pan over low heat until it becomes a rich golden brown. Pour immediately into the baking pan before it burns, spreading it over the bottom.

Put the remaining ¼ cup of sugar, the milk, eggs and candy caps in the blender and puree until smooth. Pour into the pan on top of the caramelized sugar. Place the baking pan in the oven in the larger pan with the water. Bake for 45 minutes to an hour, or until set in the center. Check by shaking the pan lightly to see if it is fluid or set. If you see any bubbling of the flan through the glass, remove it from the oven immediately, or it will toughen and separate. If it is not yet set, turn the oven down to 250 or 275° F, and finish at the lower temperature.

Candy Cap Whipped Cream, 1

This is a delicious topping for most desserts, fruit, hot chocolate, hot cider, etc. If you have candy cap syrup on hand, it is quick and easy to make, but less stable than the following recipe.

Makes about 1½ cups

½ pint whipping cream

3 to 4 tablespoons candy cap syrup, (see recipe on page 219)

Chill all ingredients, and the bowl and beater, for fastest results.

Pour the cream into a bowl, and beat it until it thickens and forms soft peaks. Add candy cap syrup, a tablespoonful at a time (to taste), beating between each addition. Beat until stiff, being careful not to over-beat and turn it to butter!

Candy Cap Whipped Cream, 2

This method is lengthier, but produces a more stable cream that will separate less easily.

Makes about 1½ cups

½ pint whipping cream

2 tablespoons ground dried candy caps

1 to 4 tablespoons sugar, to taste

In a small saucepan, heat the cream, mushrooms and sugar until they are good and hot, but not quite to a simmer. Allow to cool to room temperature, then chill for at least 2 hours. Chill the bowl and beater, also.

When chilled, beat the cream mixture until it is stiff, being careful not to over-beat.

Candy Cap-Honey Whipped Cream

This has a richer flavor, though not as obviously candy cap, than using candy cap syrup or ground candy caps. It is delicious as a topping or to frost a cake.

Makes about 1½ cups

1 cup whipping cream

4 tablespoons candy cap honey, or to taste (see recipe on page 220)

Whip the cream until it just begins to thicken. Stir in candy cap honey to taste, and continue to beat until the cream is stiff. Do not over-beat or it can separate.

Candy Cap Cream Pie

For a butterscotch version, substitute the pudding recipe on page 230, and use a 9-inch crust

Makes 8 servings.

1 baked 8-inch pie crust (see recipe on page 253)

1 recipe candy cap pudding (see recipe on page 229)

1 cup whipping cream

3 tablespoons candy cap syrup (see recipe on page 219)

Fill the pie shell with the warm pudding and chill. When pie is cold, add the candy cap syrup to the cream and whip until stiff. Cover top of pie with whipped cream.

Optional garnish: minced candied candy caps (see recipe on page 250)

Candy Cap Pumpkin Pie

Serves 8

1 cup milk

2 tablespoons brown sugar

½ cup sugar

¼ cup dried or ½ cup fresh candy caps

1 teaspoon cinnamon

½ teaspoon ginger

¼ teaspoon nutmeg

3 eggs

2 cups pumpkin, cooked

9-inch pie shell (see recipe on page 253)

Preheat the oven to 350° F. Put the milk, sugars, mushrooms, spices, and eggs in a blender. Add the pumpkin, pushing any chunks below the surface of the liquid, and blend. Pour into the pie shell and bake for 30 to 45 minutes, or until set in the center.

Candy Cap Pecan Pie

This recipe is for a 9-inch pecan pie, but it can be made into small tarts using a muffin tin and paper cupcake liners. To make crust for tarts, melt the butter and omit the water in the pie crust recipe, then put about a tablespoonful of dough into each paper liner, and press it into the bottom. Proceed as per the recipe, dividing the filling among the cups. Bake about 20 minutes. This pie is a little less sweet than traditional pecan pie, and has a delicious maple flavor.

Makes 1 (9-inch) pie or about 1 dozen tarts

1 unbaked pie shell, (see recipe on page 253)

½ cup butter

1½ cups candy cap syrup (see recipe on page 219)

4 eggs

¼ teaspoon salt

1½ cups broken pecan meats (walnut may be substituted)

Preheat the oven to 450° F. Prick bottom of pie crust in several places with a fork to prevent bubbling, and bake it for 15 minutes, turning every 5 minutes. Remove from the oven, and turn the oven down to 375° F.

Spread the pecans in the bottom of the pie crust. Melt the butter in a small saucepan; remove from heat, stir in the syrup and beat in the eggs and salt. Pour it over the nuts in the pie shell. Bake for 40 to 45 minutes, or until set in the center.

Candy Cap Apple Crisp

You may use other fruits in this recipe, or blend the apples with other fruits. It is excellent with half pears, or a quarter blackberries, or with a pint of huckleberries added. If you replace the apples with a juicy fruit, mix ½ cup of flour or 2 to 3 tablespoons tapioca into the fruit to thicken it. This recipe may be made vegan by using oil in place of butter and leaving out the egg, it just gives extra crunch to the crust.

Makes 16 servings

8 to 10 cups chopped apples or other fruit

¼ cup ground dried candy caps, or 1 cup fresh minced candy caps

1 teaspoon cinnamon

1 cup sugar

1 cup flour

¼ cup butter, melted

2½ cups oatmeal

1 egg (optional)

Grease a 9 by 13-inch baking pan and preheat the oven to 350° F. Mix the apples, candy caps, cinnamon and ½ cup of the sugar together and put them in the greased pan.

In a bowl, mix the remaining sugar, flour and melted butter together. Stir in the oatmeal. If you like a really crisp crust, stir in the egg, for a softer crust, toss in ¼ cup of water. For a crumbly crust, leave it dry. Sprinkle this crumble over the top of the fruit.

Bake for 45 minutes to 1 hour, or until crust is nicely browned. May be served warm or cold. May be served plain or with milk, cream, whipped cream, yogurt or ice cream.

Candy Cap Cheesecake

For an 8-inch spring-form pan, serves 12 to 16

1 cup ground pecans or almonds

1 tablespoon butter, melted

¼ cup flour or rice flour

½ cup plus 2 tablespoons sugar

1 pound cream cheese, softened

3 eggs, separated

½ cup fresh minced or 3 tablespoons dried ground candy caps

3 tablespoons lemon juice

2 cups sour cream

Preheat the oven to 325° F, with a pan of water on the bottom rack. Mix ground nuts, butter, flour and one tablespoon of the sugar to make the crust. Pat evenly into bottom of a greased spring form pan.

Mix the softened cream cheese and ½ cup of the sugar together, then stir in the egg yolks, mushrooms, lemon juice, and 1 cup of the sour cream. Beat the egg whites until stiff and gently fold ⅓ of them into the cream cheese mixture, then fold in the rest.

Seal the bottom of the spring-form pan by putting it on a sheet of foil and folding the foil up around the sides of the pan. Pour the cream cheese mixture into the cake pan. Place the cake pan on the upper rack of the preheated oven, above the pan of water. Bake for about 40 to 50 minutes, or until it has puffed up and set in the center and is just beginning to brown. Turn off the oven and allow the cheesecake to cool in the oven with the door slightly open.

When the cheesecake is cool, mix the remaining cup of sour cream and remaining 1 tablespoon of sugar together and spread over the top to hide any cracks. Enjoy!

Honey Oatmeal Candy Cap Cake

Recipe from Cynthia Frank.

Cake:

1 cup regular rolled oats (not the quick-cooking ones)

1¼ cup hot water

1¾ cups whole wheat flour

¼ cup ground, dried candy cap mushrooms

1 teaspoon baking soda

¼ teaspoon baking powder

¼ teaspoon ground nutmeg

¾ teaspoon salt

1 teaspoon cinnamon

1½ cups light-flavored honey

1 teaspoon vanilla

½ cup melted butter

2 large eggs

Topping:

½ cup melted butter

¾ cup honey

2 cups shredded unsweetened coconut

pinch of salt

Preheat oven to 350° F.

Grease a 9 × 9-inch square baking pan.

Soak the oats in the hot water for 20 minutes in a large bowl.

In a separate bowl, mix the whole wheat flour with the ground mushrooms, baking soda, baking powder nutmeg, salt, and cinnamon.

Whisk honey, vanilla, melted butter, and eggs into the oats one ingredient at a time.

Stir in the flour mixture until just combined and pour into the greased baking pan.

Bake for 30 to 40 minutes, until the top springs back. (It's okay if the top cracks.)

While the cake is baking, combine melted butter and honey with coconut in small saucepan. Heat until bubbly and cook for 5 minutes. Spread on baked cake while both are slightly warm.

Candy Cap Fairy Cakes

Recipe by Erif Thunen.

Special equipment needed: a mini-cupcake tin with paper inserts. Unusual ingredient: acorn flour. Acorns must be shelled, leached and ground. Pre-processed acorn flour or meal might be found in specialty shops or on the internet.

Makes 16 to 20 mini-cupcakes
⅓ cup dried candy caps
½ cup brandy
¼ cup plus 1 tablespoon butter
½ cup light brown sugar
1 small egg, beaten
¾ cup acorn flour
⅞ teaspoon baking powder
¼ teaspoon vanilla

Soak the candy caps at least 1 hour or overnight in the brandy. Drain off the brandy and reserve for another use. Sauté the candy caps in 1 tablespoon of the butter until they are dry on the surface. Allow to cool, then mince and set aside.

Preheat the oven to 375° F. Put the paper inserts into the mini cupcake pan. Cream the remaining butter and the sugar; beat in the egg and vanilla. Sift together the acorn flour and baking powder. Blend the flour into the butter mixture, then blend in the candy caps. Spoon the batter into the papers, filling them most of the way to the top—they won't rise much. Bake for 15 minutes. If your oven bakes unevenly, turn the tray around after 8 minutes. Test for doneness with a toothpick.

Candy Cap-Apple Coffeecake

Serves 9 to 12

½ cup pecans or almonds

2 cups flour

¼ cup brown sugar

½ cup butter, softened

3 to 4 apples

2 teaspoons lemon juice

½ cup candy cap syrup (see recipe on page 219)

1 teaspoon cinnamon

½ cup sugar

2 eggs

1 cup sour milk, buttermilk, or plain yogurt

1 teaspoon baking soda

½ teaspoon salt

2 tablespoons ground dried candy caps

Make the crumb crust first: chop the nuts and toast them in a dry frying pan, stirring until they begin to brown. Remove from heat, transfer to a small bowl, and allow to cool. Mix in ½ cup of the flour, and the brown sugar. Cream in 3 tablespoons of the butter until a crumbly mixture forms. Refrigerate while making the batter.

Preheat the oven to 350° F. Lightly butter an 8-inch square baking pan. Next, quarter and core the apples, then slice them thinly. Mix in the lemon juice, then the candy cap syrup and cinnamon. Set aside.

Cream remaining 5 tablespoons butter with the sugar. Beat in the eggs, one at a time. Mix in ½ cup flour, then ½ cup of the sour milk, buttermilk, or yogurt. Add another ½ cup of flour, and the remaining milk or yogurt. Finally, mix the last of the flour with the ground candy caps, baking soda and salt and mix it into the batter. Pour the batter into the prepared pan. Spread the apple slices over the top of the batter, then top with the crumb topping that has been refrigerated. Bake for about an hour or until done. Cake is done when center springs back when touched, or an inserted toothpick comes out clean.

Candy Cap Upside-Down Cake

This recipe is an old-fashioned sponge-type upside-down cake and is baked in a 9-inch or 10-inch cast iron skillet. The recipe calls for the traditional pineapple, but it's also good with apricots, peaches, mandarin oranges or apples.

Serves 12

¼ cup plus 1 tablespoon softened butter

½ cup plus 2 tablespoons candy cap syrup (see recipe on page 219)

1 (15-ounce) can pineapple rings, or 1 pint fresh fruit

1 cup pecans, walnuts or almonds (optional)

4 eggs, separated

1 tablespoon vinegar

½ cup sugar

1 cup flour (unbleached white or whole wheat pastry)

½ teaspoon baking soda

¼ teaspoon salt

2 tablespoons brandy or dark rum (optional)

Preheat the oven to 325° F. Melt ¼ cup of the butter in a 9-inch or 10-inch cast iron frying pan. Brush some of the butter up the sides of the pan. Stir in ½ cup of the candy cap syrup. Arrange the fruit and nuts decoratively in the bottom of the pan.

In a small bowl, beat the egg yolks until they are light yellow. Beat in the remaining candy cap syrup and butter.

In a large bowl, with clean beaters, beat the egg whites and the vinegar until stiff. Beat the sugar in one tablespoonful at a time. Fold in the egg yolk mixture. Sift together the flour, soda and salt and fold it in ½ cup at a time, sprinkling the flour mixture gently over the eggs and folding until just incorporated. Pour the batter gently over the fruit and bake for about ½ hour or until golden brown on top and the center springs back from a light touch. Allow to cool ½ hour, then run knife around the outside and invert the cake onto a plate. It may be sprinkled with brandy or dark rum, if desired.

Candy Cap Sticky Buns

For unsticky cinnamon rolls, omit the caramel sauce.

Makes 12 buns

Dough:

1 cup milk

¼ cup sugar

1½ teaspoons dry active yeast (½ package)

2 eggs

3 cups flour

1 teaspoon salt

½ cup butter, softened

1 extra egg for glaze

Warm the milk to around 110° F (lukewarm). Stir in 1 teaspoon of the sugar and the yeast. Allow to rest for 10 to 15 minutes, or until bubbly.

Put the yeast mixture in a large mixing bowl. Add the rest of the sugar, beat in the eggs and 1 cup of flour. Allow to rise in a warm place ½ hour. Stir in the salt and 1¼ more cups of the flour. Turn the dough out onto a floured board and knead in enough flour that the dough, while still soft, is not sticky. Oil the bowl with a light flavored oil and return the dough to the bowl. Let it rise in a warm place until double in size, about 1 to 1½ hours.

Turn the dough out onto the floured board and knead again. Roll the dough out into a square or rectangle about ¼ inch thick. Spread it with the softened butter. Fold it in half, then in half again. Wrap the dough in plastic wrap or a damp cloth and refrigerate for at least 1 hour or overnight. While the dough chills, make the filling and the caramel sauce.

Candy Cap Filling for Cinnamon Rolls

½ cup butter, softened

½ cup brown sugar

2 tablespoons dried ground candy cap mushrooms

1 teaspoon cinnamon

½ teaspoon cardamom (optional)

1 cup chopped toasted pecans, almonds, or walnuts

½ cup raisins (optional)

Blend the butter, sugar, spices and ground candy caps by hand or in a food processor. If the nuts are not roasted, toast them in a dry skillet over medium heat, stirring frequently.

The butter mixture should be soft for spreading, and the nuts and raisins kept separate for scattering onto the filling.

Caramel Sauce

¼ cup butter

1 cup cream

1 cup candy cap syrup (see recipe on page 219)

¼ cup honey

½ teaspoon salt

¼ teaspoon grated lemon rind

Melt the butter in a saucepan. Stir in the cream, candy cap syrup, honey, lemon rind and salt. Stirring constantly, bring to a boil, then simmer, continuing to stir, until glaze becomes light golden brown, about 10 to 15 minutes. (If cooked too long the butter will separate out. If this happens, remove it from the heat immediately. It may be used anyway as the butter will absorb into the rolls during and after the cooking.)

Assembly

When the dough has finished chilling, knead it once more and roll it out to a rectangle 18 inches long and ¼ inch thick. Spread the filling on the dough, leaving 1 inch along one of the long sides unfilled. Sprinkle with the nuts and raisins. Beat the remaining egg with ½ teaspoon of water. Brush a little of the egg along the unfilled edge. Reserve the rest for glazing the top before baking.

Starting at the edge opposite the side with the egg wash, roll the dough into an 18-inch-long log. Slice the log into 12 pieces, each 1½ inches wide. Grease a 9 by 13-inch pan and pour about ½ of the caramel sauce into the bottom of the pan, spreading it evenly. Lay the roll slices in the pan, evenly spaced in a 4 by 3 pattern. Allow them to rise in a warm place until doubled in size (1 to 2 hours depending on how long it was chilled). Preheat the oven to 350° F, after the dough has partially risen.

When rolls have risen, brush them lightly with the rest of the beaten egg wash. Bake them for 45 minutes to 1 hour, or until the buns are golden brown and the filling is bubbling. Remove them from the oven and spoon the remaining caramel sauce evenly over the top. Let them cool in the pan. Serve them warm or at room temperature.

Candy Cap Baklava

This recipe should be made at least a day before serving. Take the phyllo dough out of the freezer the night before. Have ready a 9 by 13-inch pan and a pastry brush. Many baklava recipes use bread crumbs as a binder for the nuts; this recipe uses apples for a moister filling.

Makes 24 pieces.
1 pound frozen phyllo dough sheets, thawed over night in the refrigerator
1 to 1½ pounds nuts: almonds, walnuts, pecans, pistachios or a blend
2 to 3 cooking apples (2 cups minced)
1 cup dried or 2 cups fresh candy caps
½ cup sugar
1 teaspoon cinnamon
½ teaspoon ground cardamom

1 cup butter, melted

1½ cups candy cap honey (see recipe on page 220)

1½ cups candy cap syrup (see recipe on page 219)

Chop the nuts (if using more than one kind, process each type separately because of different hardnesses) in a food processor until they are minced, but stop before they become a meal or paste. Move to a large bowl. Chop the apples in the food processor until they are finely chopped; add to the nuts. Chop the candy caps in a food processor if fresh, or if dried in a blender, spice mill or coffee grinder until they are minced or ground. Mix the nuts, apples, mushrooms, sugar and spices together. Preheat the oven to 350° F.

Cut the phyllo dough sheets in half crosswise, so the sheets will fit the pan. Lay the stack of sheets on plastic or waxed paper, and cover the whole pile with plastic or a barely damp towel. As you work with each sheet of dough, keep the rest of the pile covered, so it doesn't dry out.

Brush the bottom and sides of the pan with melted butter. Lay down 10 sheets of phyllo dough, brushing butter between each sheet. Spread ⅓ of the nut mixture over this. Then add 7 more sheets of phyllo dough, brushing butter between each sheet. (The first sheet or two of phyllo on top of the filling will want to slide around when you are trying to brush it with butter, and you'll have to hold it in place while brushing it.) Then spread half of the remaining nut mixture over the dough. Add another 7 sheets of dough, brushing butter between each sheet. Spread out the remaining nut mixture. Top with the rest of the phyllo dough, brushing butter between each sheet, and on the top.

Bake the baklava for a half hour. Remove the pan from the oven (do not turn it off) and cut the pastry into 24 triangular pieces by first cutting into 12 approximately 3-inch squares (3 pieces by 4 pieces) then cutting each into two triangles by making diagonal cuts. Put the baklava back into the oven and continue baking for another half hour, by which time it should be golden brown on top. Remove from oven and allow it to cool.

When the baklava has cooled, make the syrup by combining the honey and candy cap syrup in a sauce pan. Bring them to a boil and simmer for 5 minutes. Pour the hot syrup over the baklava. Allow it to cool completely, then cover it and allow it to sit at room temperature overnight before serving. Baklava may be stored at room temperature for up to a week.

Easy Candy Cap Ice Cream

This recipe does not require cooking a custard and cooling it before churning. Proportions of milk to candy cap syrup can be changed for a less sweet or sweeter dessert, to taste. For variations, you may add a cup of pecans or chocolate chips or raisins or almonds or whatever at the end of the churning.

Makes about 5 cups

2 cups heavy cream

1 cup milk

1 cup candy cap syrup (see recipe on page 219)

¼ teaspoon salt

Put all ingredients into an ice cream churner, and churn using the manufacturer's instructions.

Candy Cap Ice Cream

This is a traditional custard ice cream that must be cooked, then chilled, before churning. Start it at least 5 hours before serving, or start it the day before and chill overnight. For candy cap pecan ice cream, use brown sugar and add 1 cup of pecans near the end of the churning. A lower fat ice cream can be made by adjusting the proportions of milk to cream.

Makes 5 to 6 cups

2 cups milk

2 cups cream

¾ cup sugar or to taste

¼ cup dried, ground candy caps or ½ cup fresh, minced

2 eggs

¼ teaspoon salt

Put all ingredients into a saucepan and heat to a simmer, over medium-low heat, stirring constantly. Remove from heat and allow to cool to room temperature, then chill in the refrigerator. Place into an ice cream churner and churn according to the manufacturer's instructions.

Candy Cap Ice Cream, 2

This is a cooked ice cream using candy cap syrup. A lower fat version may be made by using more milk and less cream, proportionally.

Makes about one quart

½ cup candy cap syrup (see recipe on page 219)

1 pint whipping cream

½ cup milk

6 egg yolks or 2 whole eggs

Pinch of salt

Put all ingredients in a blender and blend to mix well. Put in saucepan and heat, stirring constantly with a wire whisk until the mixture thickens slightly. Cool completely, refrigerate overnight. Churn in an ice cream maker according to the manufacturer's instructions.

Easy Candy Cap-Banana Ice Cream

Other fruits can be substituted for banana. Use about 1 cup of fruit. If the fruit is tart, omit the lemon, and increase the syrup if desired. For a chunky fruit ice cream, mash or purée half of the fruit, and chop the rest, adding the chopped at the end of the churning cycle.

Makes about a quart

1½ cups heavy cream

3 bananas, mashed

¾ cup candy cap syrup (see recipe on page 219)

¼ teaspoon salt

Combine all ingredients in an ice cream churner and churn according to the manufacturer's instructions.

Candy Cap Cantaloupe Sorbet

This recipe can be made with other fruits, such as peaches or pineapple, or with orange or apple juice. Use 3 to 4 cups of fruit or fruit juice, and adjust the candy cap syrup to taste. Omit the lemon for acidic fruit.

Makes about a quart, depending on the size of the fruit

1 cantaloupe

1 cup candy cap syrup or to taste (see recipe on page 219)

1 tablespoon lemon juice

¼ teaspoon salt (optional)

Remove the peel and seeds from the cantaloupe, and chop it. Put it into a blender with all other ingredients and purée. (Some fruit may be retained and chopped, and added near the end of churning for a chunky version.) Chill the purée in the refrigerator for two hours, then churn in an ice cream churner according to the manufacturer's instructions.

Candy Cap Peach Parfait

This can be made with peaches, berries, cantaloupe or other melon, pears, etc. You may also blend peaches and raspberries for a peach melba version.

Serves 4

2 cups broken ladyfingers or diced angel food cake

2 cups peeled chopped peaches (or other fruit), plus 4 nice slices for a garnish

1 pint of vanilla, caramel or candy cap ice cream

½ cup whipping cream

⅝ cup candy cap syrup (see recipe on page 219)

If using angel food cake, toast it in a 375° F oven for 10 minutes. Whip the cream, whipping in 2 tablespoons candy cap syrup. Layer, in 4 parfait glasses, the ladyfingers or cake, the fruit and the ice cream, using about ¼ cup per layer. Spoon 2 tablespoons candy cap syrup over each dessert, top with whipped cream and garnish with fruit.

Candy Cap Soufflé

Serves 6

4 eggs

4 tablespoons butter

4 tablespoons flour

½ cup candy cap syrup (see recipe on page 219)

½ cup half-and-half, or cream

¼ teaspoon salt

¼ teaspoon cream of tartar

Separate the eggs, put the whites aside and beat the yolks.

Melt the butter in a saucepan. Stir in the flour. Heat it until it's bubbly. Stir in the candy cap syrup and half-and-half or cream. Cook it, stirring constantly, until the sauce thickens. Beat the egg yolks in with a wire whisk. Cook, stirring, for one minute. Remove from heat and allow to cool completely.

Preheat the oven to 325° F. Whip the egg whites, salt and cream of tartar in a clean bowl with a clean egg beater until stiff and shiny. (Any trace of egg yolk on the beater will prevent the whites from beating well.) Gently fold ⅓ of the egg whites into the sauce to lighten it. Then fold in the rest, very gently. Do not over mix; a few streaks are acceptable. Pour into an ungreased 7-inch soufflé pan or 2 ramekins, and bake for 10 minutes, then turn the heat up to 350° F, and bake 20 minutes more, or until golden, puffed, and set in the centers. Do not open the oven for the first 20 minutes of cooking time to allow the rising of the soufflés and to prevent premature collapse. Serve hot or cold with whipped cream and candy cap syrup.

Candied Candy Caps

This is a way of preserving candy caps and making a candy. They can be eaten plain, or dipped in a chocolate coating (by melting bar chocolate or chocolate chips) or chopped and added to cereals, trail mix, etc. They need to be stored in an air-tight container, as over time they will absorb moisture from the air and get sticky.

Makes about 1 cup

1 cup sugar

½ cup water

1 cup fresh candy caps

Mix the sugar and water in a sauce pan. Add the candy caps and bring to a boil. Cover and simmer for 20 minutes.

Pick the mushrooms out of the syrup with a fork (reserving the syrup) and put them on a sheet of waxed paper on a food dehydrator rack or cookie sheet. Dry overnight in a dehydrator, or in an oven with a pilot light, or dry for a couple hours on the lowest setting of an oven. They should feel dry and be hard but chewy when they are done.

The reserved syrup may be used for repeated batches of mushrooms, using fewer mushrooms, so they are still covered by the syrup. If the syrup thickens too much, add a little water to replace that which evaporated out during boiling.

Candy Cap Opera Creams

Reminiscent of maple sugar candy, these creams evoke childhood memories of Vermont winters. An accurate candy thermometer makes this recipe easier.

Makes about a pound

½ cup packed fresh candy caps or ¼ cup dried

¾ cup whipping cream

1 cup milk

⅛ teaspoon (or less) salt

2 cups sugar

Put the mushrooms, milk, cream, and salt in blender (if using dried mushrooms, allow this mixture to soak for ½ hour), and purée until smooth.

Put the sugar in a heavy saucepan and add mushroom and milk mixture. Bring to a boil, stirring until the sugar is dissolved. Cover and turn down the burner. Simmer about 3 minutes until the steam has washed down any crystals on the sides of the pan. Uncover and boil over low heat to the soft-ball stage, 234° F. (Expect to burn the bottom of your pan.)

Remove from heat. Cool to 110° F. Beat mixture until creamy. Pour it into special rubber sheet candy molds or a buttered pan. When cold, cut into squares or scoop with a spoon and roll into balls, or remove from molds. Place into an airtight container. This candy improves if aged at least 24 hours. When it has ripened, you may dip it in a chocolate coating, if desired.

Candy Cap Truffles

Makes about a pound

2 tablespoons ground dried candy caps

½ cup whipping cream

½ pound white chocolate

2 tablespoons cocoa butter

½ cup unsalted butter

3 tablespoons minced toasted nuts: almonds, hazelnuts or pecans, or

3 tablespoons cocoa powder for coating

In a small bowl, mix the candy caps into the cream.

Melt the white chocolate, cocoa butter and butter in a bowl or double boiler, over boiling water, on the stove. As soon as the chocolate is melted, mix in the cream and candy caps. Continue to stir the mixture over the boiling water for 15 minutes. Then allow to cool, stirring occasionally until it thickens.

When it reaches room temperature, refrigerate it until it's firm enough to roll into balls, about 2 hours. Scoop out ½ inch chunks with a spoon, roll them between your hands into balls, and then roll them in the finely chopped nuts or cocoa powder. Refrigerate until serving.

Miscellaneous

Pie Crust

Makes one 8 or 9-inch pie shell (for a 2 crust pie double the recipe)
1 cup flour
⅜ cup butter
½ teaspoon salt
¼ teaspoon nutmeg (optional)
A few tablespoons water

If the pie shell is to be pre-baked, preheat the oven to 450° F.

Smash the butter into the flour, salt, and nutmeg with a fork or pastry cutter until the flakes vary in size from lentil sized to cornmeal sized. Very gently, with the fork, toss in water, a spoonful at a time, until the smallest flakes are lentil sized.

Lay out a pastry cloth or a smooth dishtowel on the counter and flour it lightly. Turn out the dough onto the prepared surface, and gently, without compressing it too much, gather the dough together into a disk shape. Roll it out with a floured rolling pin, using as little flour as possible, but enough to prevent sticking, into a 12-inch diameter circle. (For an 8-inch pie, roll out to 10 inches.)

Lay the pie pan upside down on it, and place your hand under the cloth, and invert. Pull off the pastry cloth or towel, gently push the dough into the bottom of the pan, and fold the edge of the dough under to even it with the edge of the pie pan, and crimp the edge.

If required, bake for about 15 minutes, turning every 5 minutes.

Beefsteak Jerky

Recipe by Teresa Sholars.

   1 cup orange juice

   1 cup soy sauce

   1 beefsteak mushroom, sliced ⅛ to ¼-inch thick

Mix together the orange juice and soy sauce in a medium-sized bowl. Add the sliced mushroom. Push all the mushroom pieces down into the marinade if possible. (If the mushroom is too large, stir the pieces in the marinade to coat them all, then stir them several times during the marinating, to marinate all pieces evenly.) Marinate for 2 to 4 hours. Lay the slices out on the screens of a dehydrator and dehydrate overnight or until dry. They may also be dried on parchment paper in an oven with a pilot light or on its lowest setting with the door open, or on parchment paper on a screen over a heater or wood stove. (Parchment paper will prevent drips, but you should turn the mushroom slices half-way through drying.)

Cauliflower Mushroom Pasta

Cauliflower mushroom may be boiled and served with any pasta sauce, but its delicate flavor is best suited to light sauces, pesto or dressing it with oil or butter, a little garlic and fresh herbs, and parmesan.

   1 large cauliflower mushroom (*Sparassis crispa*)

Clean the mushroom thoroughly and trim off any tough parts near the stem. Cut it into chunks. Put them into a large sauce pan and cover them with water. Bring to a boil, turn down to a simmer and cover. Simmer 10 to 20 minutes or until the mushroom is tender. Drain and serve with any pasta sauce, pesto, or just olive oil, garlic and Parmesan cheese.

If using a tomato sauce, it may be simmered in the sauce for a few minutes, after parboiling, if desired.

Smoked Mushrooms

Smoking in a Barbeque

One way to smoke mushrooms is to use a Weber type barbecue, cooking on charcoal and soaked wood for the smoke. Soak some hardwood (I use old oak wine barrel planter staves) in water for about an hour while you light the fire and prepare the mushrooms. When the coals are hot, shove them to one side of the barbecue, lay the wet wood atop the hot coals, and place the grill on the fire.

Place the mushrooms on the grate on the opposite side of the grill from the hot coals, and let them cook over the indirect heat. Cover the barbecue and allow the mushrooms to smoke for 5 to 10 minutes. (You can also do a nice smoked chicken this way. You'll have to cook the chicken about an hour.)

Smoking in a Wood Stove

If you use wood heat, you may place the mushrooms in a metal can or bowl, or make a bowl shape out of heavy-duty aluminum foil. Build a small fire, or let the fire die down, and shove the wood to the back or side. Put the can or bowl of mushrooms in the space you made in the wood stove, and damp the stove down as much as possible. Allow to smoke for 5 to 15 minutes, depending on how hot or smoky the stove is.

Uses

When smoked, the mushrooms may be used fresh, or dried for later use. Boletes and many other mushrooms dry and reconstitute well. Pig's ears are best used fresh. They can be dried for storage, but they are tough reconstituted, and need a long stewing, or may be powdered in a coffee grinder or spice mill to use.

To dry smoked mushrooms, slice them and dry in dehydrator at 115° F. Mushrooms will take varying times to dry, depending upon how thickly they are sliced.

Dried Mushrooms

Slice the mushrooms, if they are large, and dry in food dehydrator at 105° F until they are crisp (overnight will usually be enough). Small mushrooms, like candy caps, may be dried whole. Dry candy caps at 90° F.

Another option is to use your oven at the lowest temperature, or with the pilot light only. This may take from 4 to 8 hours, depending upon how thickly the mushrooms are cut.

Remove the mushrooms from the dehydrator or oven when they are completely dry, and allow them to cool to room temperature. Store them in moisture-proof containers, such as glass jars. Mushrooms stored in plastic bags may mold or get bugs over time.

Smoky Porcini Salt

A seasoning useful in many savory dishes which you may customize with your own favorite herbs.

Use any amount of dried smoked Porcini mushrooms, Sea salt or Himalayan salt or any personal favorite salt.

Grind mushrooms in spice grinder and mix with salt to make a seasoning mix. Vary the proportions of salt to mushrooms according to your taste, starting with a small ratio of salt.

Feel free to add herbs such as garlic powder, turmeric, cumin, onion, oregano, dried parsley or thyme to customize your blend.

Mushroom Salts

This seasoning is easy to make and adds great dimension and flavor to many dishes.

Dried *Boletus edulis*, or any of the boletes, or try other mushrooms.

Sea salt (to taste)

Grind them in a blender or coffee grinder and add a bit of salt, to taste. Try adding garlic, toasted sesame seeds, or oregano, or dried powdered seaweed for variety. Sprinkle onto soups, baked potatoes, salads or popcorn, or use as a condiment at the table.

Gaia Blend

An elemental concoction of sea vegetable, salt, fungus, fire, seeds. A table seasoning for eggs, salads, vegetables, soups, potatoes, pizza, or canapés: finger pinching good.

Ground dried seaweed

Your favorite sea salt or Himalayan salt

Ground dried (smoked, optional) mushrooms

Toasted sesame seeds

Combine these ingredients in proportions to your taste. Experiment with adding cumin, oregano, garlic, or other herbs.

Candy Cap Seasoning

Recipe by Irina Valioulina.

Makes ¼ cup

2 tablespoons ground dried candy caps

2 tablespoons ground dried oyster mushrooms

Combine the two mushroom powders. Use this blend as a seasoning on vegetables, meat or pasta.

Chicken Rub

1 part turmeric

1 part garlic granules

1 part mushroom salt (see recipe on page 257)

1 part baharat* (optional) (recipe follows)

Brine the poultry by immersing it in salted water (1 cup salt per gallon of water) in the refrigerator for one or more hours before cooking. Pat it dry and massage the chicken rub all over the meat. Roast as usual.

Baharat

Baharat is a Middle Eastern spice blend, a mixture of the following ingredients:

4 parts black pepper

3 parts coriander seeds

3 parts cinnamon

2 parts cloves

4 parts cumin seeds

1 part cardamom pods

3 parts nutmeg

6 parts paprika

Toast the coriander and the cumin seeds before grinding them. Grind all the spices very finely together. The mixture can also be mixed with olive oil and lime juice to form a marinade.

Recommended Reading

Mushrooms Demystified, 1986, by David Arora, Ten Speed Press. This is the ultimate mushroom book for California; it covers mushrooms nationwide, but California mushrooms are covered best. The keys are fairly easy to use with practice. If you have a mushroom and you don't know what it is, this will tell you. Some of the names are outdated.

All That the Rain Promises and More, 1991, by David Arora, Ten Speed Press. This pocket guide does not have all the mushrooms you might encounter; the rudimentary key is only to group, but it has most of the mushrooms used in this book, and color, glossy pictures. It is of a convenient size to take out on the field. It's quite good for the novice learning what to eat and what not to eat.

Mushrooms of the Pacific Northwest, 2009, by Steve Trudell and Joe Ammirati, Timber Press, Inc. This book also has excellent color pictures, and is more recent than Arora's books, but it is focused north of California. Most mushrooms in northern California are in this book, but not all. The keys in this book are only to genus.

Index